Adam Zwar is an actor, writer and voice artist. He is the co-creator of the Australian comedy series *Squinters*, *Lowdown* and *Wilfred*, created the Channel 10 comedy series *Mr. Black* and the factual series *Agony Aunts*, *Agony Uncles*, *The Agony of Life*, *The Agony of Modern Manners* and *Agony*. He also presented and produced the cricket documentaries *Underarm: The Ball that Changed Cricket* and *Bodyline: The Ultimate Test*, and hosts the podcast '10 Questions with Adam Zwar'.

ADAM ZWAR

Twelve Summers

Being a life-long fan of Australian cricket is harder than it looks

hachette AUSTRALIA

Published in Australia and New Zealand in 2021
by Hachette Australia
(an imprint of Hachette Australia Pty Limited)
Level 17, 207 Kent Street, Sydney NSW 2000
www.hachette.com.au

10 9 8 7 6 5 4 3 2 1

A catalogue record for this
book is available from the
National Library of Australia

ISBN: 978 0 7336 4738 3 (paperback)

Cover design by Peter Long
Cover photograph courtesy of Allstar Picture Library Ltd/Alamy
Author photograph by Ben King
Typeset in Bookman Old Style by Kirby Jones
Printed and bound in Australia by McPherson's Printing Group

'It is the most shattering experience of a young man's life when one morning he awakes and quite reasonably says to himself, "I will never play the Dane."' – Uncle Monty, *Withnail and I*

For Amanda. You helped shape this pile of words and saved me from myself. I'm forever grateful for your wisdom and patience. And your love of cricket!

For Dad. You taught me the power of a lean sentence and that words can be a force for good. By the way, it's difficult for me to be out LBW if I'm that far forward.

For Mum. You taught me empathy and determination and encouraged me to lead a creative life. I'm so sorry you never got to meet Amanda. Or see anything I made that wasn't a disaster.

Contents

Preface 1

1. 1980–81 Australian Summer and Underarm 5
2. My First ODI and the 1987 World Cup 27
3. The 1992 World Cup and Goodbye to Border 55
4. Dean Jones and Australia A 72
5. The 1996 World Cup 92
6. The 1999 Tour of the West Indies 116
7. The 1999 World Cup 133
8. The 2001 Tour of India 150
9. 2001 Ashes Tour of England 177
10. 2002–3 Ashes in Australia 203
11. 2005 Ashes Tour of England 227
12. 2006–7 Ashes in Australia 251

Epilogue 275

Acknowledgements 289

Sources 290

'Yorkshire 232 all out. Hutton ill.
No, I'm sorry – Hutton 111.'
– commentator John Snagge

Getting the cricket stats right for this book was always going to be a challenge. The reporting on individual games can sometimes differ from the scorecard, and one scorecard can differ from another. So I was careful to triple check. But more challenging than stats, are facts. Along the way, I discovered that Langer was hit in the arm from Steve Harmison's *second* ball at Lord's in the 2005 Ashes, not his first. It's 'Adelaide Oval', not 'The Adelaide Oval'. It's The 'Laws' of Cricket, not The 'Rules' of Cricket. And a 70-year-old Bradman didn't face Jeff Thomson in the nets at Adelaide Oval, but a 69-year-old Bradman did face him at the private house of former South Australian Cricket Association medical officer Donald Beard. I want to thank Fox Cricket statistician Lawrie Colliver for helping me out with those howlers. Writing the personal stuff was a completely different exercise as I purposely changed the names and physical descriptions of the non-public, non-family figures who crossed my path. Sometimes I turned characters into composites to add another layer of protection. So that's it. Job done. As Rodney Dangerfield said, 'I just finished my first book. Now I'm going to read another one.'

AZ, September 2021

Preface

'I was twelve when I realised I'd never play for Australia, which is obviously too young to take on that kind of grief.'

It was somewhere in the middle of the joyously disgraceful summer of 1980–81 that Allan Border was flown to Cairns to run an elite coaching clinic for kids. I was eight and not one of the kids chosen to take part, but I'd heard about the clinic because some of my friends were friends of the 'elite'. So I asked Dad if he could take me down to the Cairns Australian Football League ground to check it out, as I thought I'd be able to pick up some tips. But all I saw through the fence were a lot of kids batting in the nets and Border standing there with his arms folded. He wore dark glasses, which complemented his moustache, and, in my mind, was accompanied by an Ennio Morricone soundtrack wherever he went.

During the lunchbreak, Dad and I saw Border wandering around by himself. Dad encouraged me to ask him for an autograph, but I was too shy. So Dad and I approached 'Mr Border' together and Dad asked for an autograph on my behalf. Mr Border made the mistake of asking me how I was and I said I was fine. If I'd left it at that then the interaction would have been perfect. But I was an avid reader of the 'Star Spot' column in *Australian Cricket* magazine, so I started asking him pertinent questions, like what nickname did he prefer – Pugsley or AB, did he miss working as a clerk in the film archive department at BHP, and was his favourite drink still Tia Maria and milk. Except I pronounced it 'Tyre Mariah and milk'. Oh, how Dad and Mr Border laughed, before Dad corrected me and Mr Border placed a hand on my shoulder and told me I was a 'good kid'. That made my year – Allan Border thought I was a 'good kid'.

After that, I went home and trained with even greater verve. I pestered Dad to give me throwdowns in the backyard when he should've been working. I joined coaching clinics run by former County cricketers trying to earn a buck while backpacking around North Queensland. And whenever Australia was playing, I was watching, hoping to uncover the secret that would make me great. When I played for my club side, I opened the batting with a kid called Jimmy Maher, a compact left-hander who saw the ball early and whose fluid movements made cricket look easy. Jimmy, who'd go on to captain Queensland and represent Australia in 26 One Day Internationals, never disparaged me, but did find it perplexing that I didn't share his talents. While he'd bring up his century before lunch, I'd be lucky to be on 3, if I was still out there at all. Usually, I wasn't. Usually, I was still in my pads, sulking under a tree.

It took a couple of seasons to realise I wouldn't play for Australia. I think I just came to terms with the fact that I was better at consuming cricket than playing it. And I consumed it at a dangerously high level. I knew the nicknames of all the players, their favourite movies, drinks and meals, the last book they'd read, and whether or not they smoked. I knew the names of their wives as well. Rod Marsh was married to Ros. Greg Chappell was married to Judy. Kim Hughes was married to Jenny. And Greg Matthews was single. In fact, Greg Matthews' player profile was so honest I knew it off by heart.

Pet hates? 'Bad dudes.'

Fears? 'Failure.'

Issue you're concerned most about? 'The nuclear arms race.'

If you weren't a cricketer, what would you be doing now? 'Struggling.'

I related to Matthews. Only one of us had played for Australia, but we had both been saved by the game.

I don't know what mental state I'd be in if Australian cricket wasn't there as a banister. Sometimes I've been able to walk without it, but most of the time, I've leaned on it heavily and with both hands. It didn't matter how upset or depressed I was, or what horrible situation I'd got myself into, nothing soothed my soul quicker than Richie Benaud saying, 'Welcome to another summer.'

CHAPTER 1

1980–81 Australian Summer and Underarm

'It was an act of true cowardice and
I consider it appropriate that the Australian
team were wearing yellow.'
– New Zealand's PM Robert Muldoon

I was born in 1972. The other keen cricketer who took his first breath that year was Muttiah Muralitharan. Between us, we took 800 Test wickets at 22 apiece. But I'm getting ahead of myself.

What got me into cricket was not cricket itself, but the song 'C'mon Aussie C'mon', concocted by the deeply manipulative forces of Kerry Packer and advertising agency Mojo and sung in a lilting, 'this won't hurt a bit' tone. The idea for the anthem came from Packer's World Series Cricket consigliere John Cornell and was written by ad men Alan Morris and Al Johnston (Mojo), presumably after a four-hour lunch one afternoon in 1978. With Cornell watching on, the two Als got the guitar out, and managed to rhyme 'pickets' with 'wickets' and 'gum' with 'runs' and Graeme 'Wood' with 'good' – and within a few hours, they'd not only penned a Top 40 hit, but were well on the way to selling cricket to a new generation.

I asked Dad to record the song from the TV on his portable tape deck and while the other kids were joining the KISS Army, I played 'C'mon Aussie C'mon' over and over, and by the summer of 1980–81, cricket was all I thought about. If there was a game on television that day, my whole life revolved around the coverage. I'd have breakfast, 15 minutes of throwdowns in the backyard with Dad – who must've regretted working from home – then I'd settle down for Tony Greig's 'pitch report', followed by the toss and Ian Chappell's interviews with the captains.

One of my first memories was seeing the broadcaster's cameras catching Greg Chappell heading to the dressing room with a newspaper tucked under his arm, as if he were a businessman. Then, an hour or so later, he was striding out onto the ground in his Australian creams, going on to score a double century. Chappell looked like a school principal, so I was a bit scared of him. I found Kim Hughes more relatable. When Hughes scored a double century in the Second Test against India, I decided he was my favourite. I liked his boyish, rosy-cheeked good looks. I liked how he was nimble on his feet and often made a spectacle of dancing down the wicket just to block. According to *Australian Cricket* magazine, Kim Hughes was an Aquarian who worked as a building society officer. His favourite food was a pepper steak, his favourite drink was a brandy and dry, favourite movie – *Rocky III*, favourite magazine – *Playboy*. He liked barbecues and sincere people and disliked armchair critics and false people. Some might wonder how Hughes beat out Lillee and Marsh to be my favourite, and all I can say is at the age of eight, Hughes was my gateway drink, a shandy to the neat Jack Daniels of Dennis Lillee and Rod Marsh. They were something to be appreciated later.

I lived in a fantasy world where the Australian cricket team dressing room was a happy place full of friendship and bonhomie, with everyone in a constant state of delight at being able to play cricket for their country. The reality was the team was overworked, underpaid and at the point of exhaustion. By February '81, Australia had played 15 Tests in 14 months – at home, in Pakistan and England – and 21 One Day Internationals. The team had a manager, but no coach or support staff. Sometimes there wasn't even a physio. Most things fell onto Greg Chappell's shoulders. He was responsible for organising the team's training and travel arrangements. He held press conferences and met with officials to discuss programming, player payments and poor pitches. And then he'd have to score runs, unpick opposition weaknesses and come up with a tactical plan to approach each game.

When I made a documentary on the era 30 years later, Chappell said that in early 1981, he was on the verge of a nervous breakdown.

'I was struggling to sleep,' he said. 'I was struggling to eat. And it was starting to really affect my ability to perform. But I've always been a strong-willed character, I suppose, so I just kept pushing myself and pushing myself. And pretending that it wasn't an issue. But obviously it was an issue because it all bubbled up on the MCG on February the 1st.'

On that boiling hot Melbourne Sunday, Australia and New Zealand were one–all going into the third final of the best-of-five World Series Cup.

Chappell had made it clear to his team that they had to win the match to limit the series to four games. He told them if they won that day, and the fourth final in Sydney on Tuesday, the team would avoid having to play a fifth final and therefore have a much-needed three days off before the Third Test against India. It was this desperate need to have an extra day off that brought about the single most talked about incident in the history of cricket.

New Zealand Prime Minister Robert Muldoon would call it 'an act of true cowardice'. Richie Benaud would call it 'one of the worst things I have ever seen done on a cricket field'. And Bill Lawry would call it 'possibly a little bit disappointing'.

It was underarm.

Mr White

Being a kid was a bit of a drag for me because I was unpopular at school. Whenever I joined a new club or sporting organisation, I'd be excited because it was a chance to meet kids who didn't know I was meant to be teased. But they'd somehow get the memo because I'd end up being teased wherever I went. Forty years later, I can see the orange hair, pageboy do, chipped front tooth and homemade brown towelling shirt and short pants combo hindered my progress. But I didn't know that then. I just thought being an outcast was a cruel twist of fate and one day, everyone would come to their senses. Meanwhile, cricket was a sanctuary – the commentators were my rogue uncles and the players, my big brothers.

My home was in Cairns, Queensland. We had a house on a hill. I was an only child and we had a cat called Pushpa – a Hindi word meaning 'little flower'. Mum and Dad were well-known in Cairns circles. Everyone loved Mum, a cordon bleu cook who became a food and lifestyle writer for *Gourmet Traveller* and *House and Garden*. I'd hear her transcribe interviews in her office and you could tell every self-important chef and interior designer she interviewed adored her. She had such an empathetic ear and the ability to make them feel whole. Whereas Dad was a controversialist. He was an Aussie journalist who'd conquered Fleet Street and become a bestselling author. He smoked cigars, drank red wine and would see your dinner party anecdote and raise it. He was great with accents too. People would sit enthralled as this thickly set bald man told stories about meeting the first man in space, Yuri Gagarin; how he'd sat on the toilet of Hitler's deputy Rudolf Hess in Spandau Prison; and played golf with Sean Connery. I knew all Dad's stories by heart, and if he were to drop dead mid-anecdote, I was confident I could land the ending on his behalf. Dad was also an amateur cop. If our neighbours' music was too loud or their dog barked at night, they could expect a knock on the door from Dad. He didn't care what anyone thought of him.

Then there was 'Mr White', the belt Dad whacked me with when I answered back, had a tantrum, or got in a fist fight with my next-door neighbour over his inability to grasp the subtleties of the LBW rule. 'Go and get Mr White,' Dad'd say. So I would. Then he'd wrap the top part of the belt around his hand and say, 'This'll hurt me more than it hurts you.' And he'd whack me three times in a row on my bum and around my legs. One night, he attended a Parents and Friends Association seminar on disciplining children. The guest speaker talked about 'negotiating' with your child. Dad told the gathering he didn't worry about any of that, he just used Mr White. The speaker walked straight into his trap by asking who Mr White was and Dad proudly told him. The meeting descended into chaos, but Dad didn't care. He wasn't bothered by conflict.

As you walked into Dad's home office, the first thing you'd see, hanging on the wall, were the framed covers of all the books he'd written, including *The Loneliest Man in the World* (about Hess), *The Infamous of Nuremberg* (about the Nuremberg trials) and, in a departure from theme, *This Wonderful World of Golf,* for which he'd accompanied five-time British Open winner Peter Thomson on the golf tour for a year. Dad would joke that after Thomson, Arnold Palmer, Jack Nicklaus, Gary Player and Lee Trevino all 'helped' him with his swing – he went from a serviceable 14 handicap to a shanking 21.

On the opposing wall were shelves of books, and sitting on top of the shelves was a rifle. Dad told me he used to be a representative target shooter, but I never thought anything of it. There were no guns in cricket, so what was the point of them? Then, one night, during a long dinner party, there was a stand-off in the front yard between our cat, Pushpa, and a taipan. The taipan had risen up to Pushpa and their heads were level and only inches apart. Dad saw the stand-off, left the dinner table, and returned with his rifle. He put it to his shoulder and aimed. It was a difficult shot. Not only was it dark, but he was standing 20 metres from Pushpa and the snake. To make matters worse, Pushpa had crept even closer to the snake. I was petrified. We were a small family – just Mum, Dad, Pushpa and me. We'd lost Herby the hermit crab only a few months earlier and couldn't afford to lose anyone else. Mum asked Dad if he was sure he was doing the right thing. She and the guests were still sitting at the table, casting their eyes nervously between Dad and the animals. Dad slowly squeezed the trigger. *Bang*. We looked out … Pushpa was still standing, but the taipan was now without its head. Dad went back to the dinner table and resumed his anecdote about tracking down the Dalai Lama via phone when he was in exile.

'Is that the Dalai Lama?' he said, mocking his own Australian accent. 'It's Desmond Zwar here from the *Dalai Mail*.' Cue raucous laughter.

Dad was a hero to me. Embarrassingly, he was always the first parent waiting at the school gate to pick me up and he'd bowl to me in the backyard, acutely aware I didn't have a sibling. Or friends. The parents of the neighbour I used to play cricket with had banned us from hanging out when they discovered the Zwars were not Roman Catholic. I occasionally spent time with a kid called Quan when our parents had dinner parties. I liked him because he owned his eccentricity whereas I was trying to hide mine. Quan was obsessed with kung-fu and didn't like dogs – 'Dogs give me rash, man.' I remember Quan being crouched in a kung-fu pose as the neighbour's Dalmatian approached, wagging its tail. 'Back off, man,' he told the dog. 'Or I'll be forced to do something I'll regret.' I lost touch with Quan when his family moved away. He would come back into my life 20 years later with the power to save my career. But right now, the friend cupboard was bare and Dad was concerned about me crying all the time. I can't remember if the crying was because I was upset over specific things, like Australia losing an ODI, or general things, like being alive. In any case, Mum and Dad took me to a child psychologist. I waited outside the psychologist's office while my parents briefed her on my condition and I heard the psychologist say, 'Have you any theories on what's making Adam so upset?' There was a brief silence, then Dad said, 'He does eat a lot of honey.'

After five sessions with the psychologist, she recommended that some time away camping might improve my mood. Dad wasn't that interested in the great outdoors, but, on doctor's orders, he took me camping on the Atherton Tablelands. He asked a friendly Italian tobacco farmer if we could camp on his property by the river and the farmer said that'd be fine. So we made our way down a steep gully and set up our tent next to the river, which bordered an avocado farm. It was an idyllic afternoon. We started fishing and it didn't take long before I had a fish on the hook, but halfway through reeling it in, the fish managed to wriggle itself free. So I said, 'Cunty fish,' thinking there was comedy in turning a swear noun into an adjective.

Dad didn't see it like that. 'WHAT DID YOU SAY?' he said, his face turning red.

I started to explain my comedic approach, but I could see he was in no mood for explanations. So I bolted. But Dad had some pace on him and was able to grab me and bring me down. Then, just as I was about to receive a hiding, the friendly Italian tobacco farmer who'd let us camp on his property opened fire on the avocado farmer who lived on the other side of the river. And the avocado farmer fired right back at him. Bullets from 303s whistled over our heads. Dad understood a smattering of Italian and told me they were arguing about the boundary of their properties and to keep my head down. He then got up, took off his shirt, waved it at the gunmen, and yelled, 'I HAVE AN EIGHT-YEAR-OLD DOWN HERE!'

They stopped. We packed the tent away and went home. Fortunately for me, the shootout became the story we told Mum. And my cunty fish misfire was never mentioned again.

Dad and I obviously had differences of opinion when it came to me working blue, but I'd always defend him when he'd write something controversial in his weekly column, 'Monday Morning with Desmond Zwar', which appeared in the *Cairns Post*. It wasn't like the kids at school had strong opinions about the column, but their parents did. And if they took issue with one of Dad's views, they'd air it at the breakfast table and then their kids would parrot these concerns in the playground – often while I was in a headlock. And then there was the day Dad went on *The Mike Walsh Show* to promote a book he'd written on newspaper proprietor Sir Keith Murdoch – the father of Rupert. For those of you not versed in the stylings of 80s Australian television, Mike Walsh was the 80s Australian version of Oprah. It was a huge opportunity for Dad and I was proud of him, but I didn't want the kids at school to know about it because any sense of me big-noting myself via Dad's prominence would lead to trouble. So when Mum dropped me off at the school gate and casually mentioned that she had told my teacher about Dad going on *Mike Walsh*, I was mortified. This would undoubtedly lead to a new round of bullying. It got catastrophically worse when my teacher told the principal about Dad's TV appearance and instead of just my class watching, the whole school was ushered into the assembly hall, with its six television screens.

On television, Dad was in a 70s-style white suit with pale blue pinstripes and flared trousers, which was still stylish in 1980s Cairns, telling the story of his car breaking down while picking up Rupert Murdoch from the airport and a neighbour giving them a lift back to our place. Dad told Mike that he'd jumped in the front seat of the neighbour's Mazda 323 while Rupert squeezed in the back with the neighbour's two-year-old daughter, who hit him over the head with her Jemima doll all the way home. The studio audience laughed. The kids in the assembly hall laughed too. That was the first time I breathed during the whole interview. After that, Mike Walsh didn't want to talk about the Murdochs anymore. He wanted to talk about Hess. But Dad still wanted to talk about the Murdochs because that was the book he was there to promote. The atmosphere between Mike and Dad got tense. The studio audience got tense. And the mood in the assembly hall got weird – as if it was my fault Dad and Mike had crossed swords. When the interview finished, I knew something was going to go down with the bullies and I'd resolved, for the first time in my life, to fight back. So when 'Rowdy' J, who had beaten me up many times in the past, pushed me and said, 'My dad thinks your dad's a dickhead', I went for him, landing several blows to his smug little face to the surprise and amusement of everyone watching. The teachers rushed to separate us, but Rowdy and I were keen to continue so we arranged to meet outside the Stratford Fire Station at 6.30 the next morning.

At dinner, Dad was full of stories about his exciting day. Normally, I'd be asking him a thousand questions, but that night I was silent and withdrawn and Mum asked Dad to find out what was wrong. Dad came into my room, sat on my bed and, after some gentle cross-examination, I told him about the fight. When he asked what had started it, I told him through tears, 'Rowdy's dad said you were a dickhead.' Dad said he didn't care what other people thought of him, but I didn't believe him. How could anyone not care about what other people thought of them?

Next morning, Dad woke me up at 6 am and drove me down to the fire station. I nervously got out of the Mini Moke and waited. And waited. By 7 am, Dad said he didn't think Rowdy would show. Before we went home, we stopped off at a milk bar to drink lemonade spiders. That's when he said he was proud of me.

1 February 1981. Underarm

On the morning of 1 February 1981, Dad and I went to church, something we did most Sunday mornings. Mum didn't go. She'd come from a religious background and felt she'd spent enough time at church for one lifetime. Dad had also come from a religious background but couldn't get enough of the place. Personally, I thought it was OK, but I didn't love it. I certainly had to play mind games to get through the 'Prayers for the People' section, which could really blow out, particularly when we'd moved on from peace in the Middle East and other life-and-death situations to praying for the return of a parishioner's lost wallet. 'Lord, hear our prayer.'

When I returned home that Sunday morning, I quickly climbed out of my brown towelling shirt and short pants and into my stubbies and T-shirt with Greg Chappell's face emblazoned on the front. I raced to the couch and turned on the telly just in time to see the Channel Nine cricket graphics accompanied by Brian Bennett's 'New Horizons', a composition intended to invoke the warmth of a sun-drenched summer which, to Australians of that era, meant cricket.

Richie Benaud welcomed viewers to the MCG for the third final in the best-of-five against New Zealand in the World Series Cup and reminded us that it was one game all. He then showed us the team cards and threw to Tony Greig down in the middle. Tony's pitch reports were my favourite part of the broadcast. Often they would start with the camera close in on Tony's ever-so-slightly flared trousers and handmade light brown leather shoes as he discussed pitch soil and grass varieties and how they were likely to impact the game. He then took us to his weather wall, a mind-blowingly futuristic device that measured wind direction, wind speed, air temperature, humidity, barometric pressure and everyone's favourite – 'The Players' Comfort Level'. Once that was out of the way, his showstopping closer was to stick his key into the pitch. Sometimes the key wouldn't break the surface ('No way in the world it'll go in'). Other times, he'd grunt and groan and force it in ('Well, that's *almost* impossible'). And then there were the times the key would go in like the pitch was warm butter ('Look at that. Straight in'). Then there was the time at the WACA when Tony lost one of his keys down a six-inch crack in the pitch and ground staff had to come out with long wire to retrieve it.

I think I liked Tony because I was an overly sensitive kid and drawn to people who seemed invincible. And no one seemed more invincible than Tony Greig. My favourite phrase of his was, 'Now, that's gone like a tracer bullet ...' If Tony agreed with a fellow commentator, then they weren't merely 'right', they were 'dead right'. Players were either 'big' like Tom Moody or 'little' like Sachin Tendulkar: 'The little man has hit the big fella for six!' Unless you were Sri Lankan, then you were always 'little': 'These little Sri Lankans ... they never give up, do they?'

As the years went by, the iconic moments piled up, like the time Steve Waugh dropped a dolly off Tendulkar: 'Straight up in the air ... Waugh won't drop this ... oh he's dropped it! I can't believe it! What's going on here?'

And then there was the shot the TV cameras captured of a beautiful female spectator dressed in a red top and headband.

Tony Greig: 'Oh boy, doesn't she look gorgeous ... Come on, Bill, say something ... He won't say anything. It's gotta be a pigeon before he comments.'

Bill Lawry: 'You dig a hole, you fill it up, mate.'

There's nothing in the world better than off-mic laughter from the comm box, particularly from the original team of Benaud, Lawry, Greig and Ian Chappell. To hear strong off-mic laughter from them was a win. Later, there'd be off-mic laughter over Warney's pizza intake, but that was comparatively cheap.

On the morning of the third final against New Zealand, Tony's analysis of the pitch was that it would play 'low and slow'. After winning the toss, Greg Chappell told his brother Ian that 'we'd have a bat', and Australia played well in the difficult conditions, making an impressive 4-235, thanks to the captain's unbeaten 90. He should've been out at 58, when he came down the pitch and mis-hit Lance Cairns over mid wicket and Martin Snedden took what appeared to be a magnificent and clean catch, but Chappell stood his ground. Since neither umpire was 'watching the ball' as it went to Snedden, they couldn't give Chappell out. I felt weird about that. It was a clean catch. Why weren't the umpires watching the ball? I was watching the ball and I was 2000 km away.

When New Zealand batted, a century from opener Bruce Edgar put the Kiwis in a winnable position. And by the final over of the match, they were 6 for 221, needing 15 to win, 14 to tie. Legendary all-rounder Richard Hadlee was on strike. According to his Star Spot profile, Hadlee's favourite car was a BMW, he had no fears or superstitions, his pet hate was stale food, he had no heroes and when asked about his favourite book, he said, 'Any of the ones I've written.' Still, he remains the best all-rounder I've seen.

Greg Chappell asked his younger brother, Trevor, to bowl the final over. His first ball was short and it didn't surprise anyone to see Hadlee give himself room and smash it past mid-on for four.

Bill Lawry: 'He's hit that. He's hit it well. Out to Max Walker and that's four ... My, what a start. Wow, 11 required for victory, five balls to be bowled.'

Trevor Chappell's next delivery rapped Hadlee on the pads. It probably pitched outside leg, but the umpire's finger shot straight up.

On an Air New Zealand aircraft carrying New Zealand Prime Minister Robert Muldoon from Wellington to Christchurch, the pilot was giving his passengers a running commentary. 'Eleven to win, four balls left.'

Kiwi wicketkeeper Ian Smith was the next to stride to the crease. No helmet, no hat, thick hair ruffling in the whirlpool MCG breeze.

Bill Lawry: 'The best they can hope for is a draw with two fours and a two. Smith's not a big hitter. It really is unfortunate that Edgar's not on strike.'

Ian Chappell: 'Well I have to disagree about Smith not being a big hitter, Bill. I saw him hit an awfully big six off Dennis Lillee at the Sydney Cricket Ground.'

Smith unconvincingly clipped the next two balls around the ground for two runs apiece.

Two balls to go and the Kiwis needed seven to win. Six to tie. Trevor Chappell proved himself a skilful death bowler when his next delivery bowled Smith, middle stump. Dennis Lillee ran from the outfield to shake Trevor's hand while the slow-motion replay showed Smith's stump leaning back and the bail twirling majestically in the air.

Ian Chappell: 'Eight down for 229. New Zealand's only hope now is to hit a six off the last ball for a tie.'

On the Air New Zealand flight, Muldoon went back to his reading materials, convinced a tie was unlikely. In Adrian McGregor's biography of Greg Chappell, he writes that the Kiwi players were ribbing their last batter, Brian McKechnie, as he put on his gloves and collected his bat. 'Don't worry about getting your eye in.' They knew a six was unlikely – the ground was too big and the wicket too slow – but McKechnie was optimistic. In the back of his mind he thought, 'You might just get a lucky blow in.'

Greg Chappell was obviously thinking along similar lines when he saw the hulking McKechnie arrive at the crease. Although the former All Black was batting at ten, Chappell believed he had the power to lift Trevor's medium pacers over the fence and put Australia's much-yearned-for day off in jeopardy.

So Greg approached his younger brother. 'How are you at bowling your underarms?' Greg asked Trevor.

'Oh, I don't know. Why?'

'Well, you're about to find out.'

It's a predictable narrative to paint Trevor as the bullied younger brother who was only following orders, but Trevor loved Greg's idea. He agreed McKechnie would struggle to hit a six off a ball rolling along the pitch.

Greg Chappell told umpire Don Weser of his plan. The eye-rolling Weser agreed to let it happen because the law banning underarm bowling, recently installed in the English cricket law book, had not yet been embraced by the Australian Cricket Board. When Weser told McKechnie that Trevor would bowl the final delivery underarm, McKechnie asked Weser if he was joking.

Rod Marsh pleaded with Greg and Trevor not to go through with it. Max Walker shook his head from deep mid-on. Ian Chappell called out from the back of the commentary box, 'No, Greg, no, you can't do that!'

Later, Greg Chappell would tell McGregor that he knew getting Trevor to bowl underarm wouldn't be received well. 'But quite honestly, I couldn't give a rat's tail,' Chappell said. 'I was quite prepared for a rap over the knuckles if it saved us from the extra game.'

The crowd, now aware of what was happening, booed as Trevor Chappell ambled toward the crease and rolled the ball along the pitch to McKechnie, who blocked it and immediately threw his bat skyward in disgust. McKechnie said he thought about trying to slog it but didn't want to be 'embarrassed' by getting bowled.

Bruce Edgar, who was at the non-striker's end, gave Trevor Chappell the forks. In the Kiwi dressing room, a player threw his cup of tea against the wall. New Zealand captain Geoff Howarth strode onto the field in his socks and with his trouser button undone to remonstrate with the umpires. They told him the delivery was legal. Kim Hughes apologised to

McKechnie and Marsh took off his glove and shook Edgar's hand.

On the New Zealand Prime Minister's flight, a nervous pilot came over the intercom after quite a few minutes of silence. 'He bowled it underarm ... and they're all arguing.'

Greg Chappell said he wasn't aware of how badly his decision had been received until he was walking off the ground. 'The kids started jumping the fence and running out,' he told our documentary, *Underarm*. 'And this young girl tugged on my shirtsleeve. And I looked down at her, and she was looking up at me and she said, "You cheated." At that moment, I'd thought that this might be a bit bigger than I'd even imagined.'

In the stand, ACB chairman Bob Parish asked Australian selector Sam Loxton, who had been crying, if he'd had a hand in Chappell's actions. Loxton responded, 'I should punch you in the nose for even asking such a thing.'

Meanwhile, a furious Richie Benaud went on air for his post-match summary and said, 'I think it was a disgraceful performance from a captain who got his sums wrong today ... One of the worst things I have ever seen done on a cricket field.' Richie explained that Chappell had intended for Lillee to bowl the final over before discovering the champion quick had already used up his allotted ten – and that's how Trevor was given the job.

When cricket fan Muldoon got off the plane in Christchurch, he waved away reporters seeking his opinion on the incident, but at midnight, a *Sydney Morning Herald* journalist rang his publicly listed number. 'Look,' Muldoon thundered, 'if the bloody Australians want it, I'll give it to you between the eyes.' And that's when he made his comment that it was appropriate the cowardly Australian team was wearing yellow.

As the cricket and political world went into meltdown, Chappell retreated. Instead of staying with the team at a hotel when they flew to Sydney that night, he joined Rod Marsh and Dennis Lillee at a secret beachside unit. When Chappell arrived there, he called his five-year-old son, Stephen. Chappell asked Stephen if he'd seen what happened. Stephen said he had. Chappell asked him what he thought, and Stephen said, 'I felt sorry for you.'

But Tony Greig was there for Chappell, castigating McKechnie for not taking the fight to the Australians. 'He didn't even try to hit the thing for six,' said Greig. 'We practised for years in England because we knew at some stage someone would bowl an underarm. For him to not run down and let it hit his toe and pop up and try and smash it for six was a gross miscalculation. Bloody atrocious.'

Australia would win the fourth final in Sydney by six wickets after a man-of-the-match winning 87 from Greg Chappell. The team got their treasured day off before playing the Third Test against India, which they'd lose on a crumbling MCG wicket.

Mum and Dad were outraged by underarm. So were our neighbours. So was Australian Prime Minister Malcolm Fraser. At school the next day, everyone was in a state of shock, but I was too in love with the game to find fault with it. My first full summer of cricket had been a revelation; there was enough personality and politics in this drama to keep me occupied for a lifetime. Even better, the more I concentrated on the fortunes of Australian cricket, the more I could escape the reality of being an average student, in a towelling suit, who got teased.

CHAPTER 2

My First ODI and the 1987 World Cup

'Border is a walnut: hard to crack and
not much to please the eye.'
– Peter Roebuck

Brendan Nash was a tidy left-hander who'd go on to play for Queensland, and then the West Indies. He came from a big Jamaican family and each Christmas his uncle would have a massive party at his place in Cairns, which I looked forward to because it was a chance to bowl at Brendan and see how much he'd improved. But my recollection from the 1984 Christmas party was that cricket had to be put on hold after I walked into the living room and saw Michael Anthony Holding AKA Mikey Holding AKA Whispering Death casually sipping a beer among the throng. My heart started beating quickly. Too quickly. I wondered if it were possible for 12-year-olds to have heart attacks. I didn't have the guts to say 'hello' to the great man, but I did stare at him for a long time before using every bit of willpower to divert my eyes and head to the kitchen. It wasn't any less intimidating there because that's where a young Courtney Walsh was holding court while mainlining on my mum's avocado dip. I poured myself a lemonade, careful not to spill it and make a scene in front of Courtney, then glanced out onto the veranda. Standing by himself, taking in the setting North Queensland sun, was the one and only, the princely Jeffrey Dujon. I knew enough to know his name was actually *Peter* Jeffrey Dujon and his nickname was Duj (pronounced *Duje*). He was a Gemini who drove a Toyota Corona and listened to soul music. He liked intelligent conversation, disliked dishonesty, and the person in the world he most wanted to meet was the person who would make him rich. It would've been so easy for me to go out on the veranda and say 'hello'. I could've asked him what Viv Richards was really like – a question I'm sure he and the rest of the West Indies team never tired of – but I wouldn't have coped if he'd rejected me. I didn't want to be in the position of turning on the television, seeing Jeff Dujon, and thinking, 'Oh, there's the guy who told me to eff off.' Not that he would have, but cricket meant way too much for me to take that chance.

For the week of my 13th birthday, we went to visit family friends in Brisbane. Their kids, who were in their late teens, took me to the Gabba to watch a one-dayer between the West Indies and Australia. This was huge. I'd never seen a live game of first-class cricket before. I was a TV guy – an observer, not a participant. I didn't know how to behave at the ground. As it turned out, there wasn't much to it. Our little group was just like everyone else except we weren't swearing or drinking. The only concession we made to fit in was to have a Four'n Twenty pie. That day, there were 22,012 people at the ground – about the population of Cairns.

Clive Lloyd won the toss and sent Australia in. Graeme Wood, Andrew Hilditch and Kepler Wessels all made starts – albeit slow ones – before getting out. Border came in to bat and was promptly hit in the 'groin' by one of Viv Richards' darting off spinners. Border spent quite a bit of time lying on the ground while Lloyd made fun of him by doing a 10-count as if the Australian skipper was a felled boxer. Moments later, Border was run-out with a direct hit by Lloyd, proving there's no such thing as justice. Simon O'Donnell, Steve Rixon and Craig McDermott were also run-out in Australia's disappointing 191. Even I knew run-outs were a sign of bad communication, and when a team had one after another, it pointed to a deeper problem.

My friends and I sat on the hill, facing the wicket side-on, which allowed me to make a discerning judgement about who was bowling fastest. As far as I could tell, Malcolm Marshall was the quickest, followed by Michael Holding and then Joel Garner. But there must've only been a handful of us in the area who gave a damn about the cricket. A lot of beer cans were being thrown and at one stage a woman in a bikini tried to kiss Geoff Lawson, who was fielding on the fence. If she'd known her cricket, she'd have known teetotaller Lawson was probably the last person willing to fool around in the middle of a One Day International.

When the Windies came out to bat, Craig McDermott, still a teenager, gave us some hope by bowling Richie Richardson and Larry Gomes in his first over. I wrote in my cricket diary that McDermott wasn't as quick as Marshall, but he probably gave Holding a run for his money. Still, any hope for an Australian miracle was snuffed out by Viv Richards and Clive Lloyd, who mauled Australia's total in 37 overs with five wickets to spare. Viv was dynamic, hitting six fours and a six in his 49. McDermott would have bowled to him at around 150 km/h, but there was never any thought of the king calling for a helmet. The guy behind me said that Viv was 'fearless'. But I'd read Viv's player profile about 50 times and knew he did fear something. He feared being 'taken for granted'.

After the game finished, we exited via the 40-metre underpass that led out onto Vulture Street. Hundreds of us were jammed in as we shuffled through the low-ceilinged passageway, all talking excitedly about Viv, and Marshall, and the shortcomings of Australian cricket. Then someone farted. Multiple XXXXs and at least two beef and burgundy pies would need to have stewed in the farter's gut for quite some time to produce an odour this rank. And instead of the fart obediently floating through the crowd before making a dignified exit, it just hung there like the Goodyear Blimp. People started grumbling and pulling their shirts up over their noses. A woman behind me leaned over and dry-retched. Meanwhile, the people up the front were taking their sweet time getting onto the street, so the rest of us started yelling at them to move quicker. But they didn't. Or wouldn't. Soon, there was pushing and shoving as the middle section of the crowd stampeded toward the exit. Some people fell over, others were run over. I managed to duck into the slipstream of some guy carrying a large esky, who was weaving his way through the throng. But even after I arrived onto the street and into the bliss of fresh air, I could still smell the fart all over me. It was in my clothes, my hair, my nostrils. If I came across that particular scent now, 36 years later, I'm certain I'd recognise it. It smelled like mid-80s Australian cricket. It smelled like defeat.

We arrived home safely and I told the adults about seeing Marshall and Viv and Lloyd and how, despite Australia's humiliating capitulation and the fart, it was the greatest day of my life and the best birthday present ever. As I was talking I noticed a man drive through the open gate of the house next door. He parked his car before getting out and closing the gate. He was a stocky little guy with a moustache, but the thing that made him seem familiar was that he carried himself with a 'fuck you' confidence rare in white guys under 5'9".

'Is that ... Allan Border?' I asked.

My friends' mother confirmed it was, and that they'd been neighbours with the Australian captain for quite a while. She then asked if I'd like to meet him.

I thought about it and wondered what I'd say. 'Hi, I'm the Tyre Mariah and milk kid.' Also, his press conference, which we had heard on the radio on the way home from the Gabba, was depressing. He'd said that Australia's first three batters should have done more and that they put too much pressure on the tailenders to score big off Marshall and Garner. And then he left us with a line that made all our hearts sink: 'As captain, I just don't know what more I can do.' So, taking into account those comments plus the fact that he'd been hit in the balls and run-out, I declined the introduction.

Years later, Border saw a play I'd written called *The Inner Sanctum*. He was part of a Cricket Australia contingent in the audience that included Mark Taylor, then CEO James Sutherland and former all-rounder Tony Dodemaide. Afterwards, Border approached the actors and asked them how they were able to recreate the nuances of what was discussed in an Australian cricket team dressing room. The actors said they didn't make the lines up and that there was a writer who wrote them. Well, Border said he wanted to meet the writer. So we were introduced. He congratulated me and said I'd got the dressing room chat just right. After a few beats of conversation, I reminded him of the time he played in a Shield game against a young Glenn McGrath, whose trousers didn't go below his shins, and Border had said, 'Hey mate, why are your pants so high? Are you expecting a flood?' He laughed. We were getting on well. Maybe Allan Border and I could be friends. I asked if he still lived in a particular Brisbane suburb.

'Y-yes,' he said, curious as to how I might know this information. Oblivious, I named the street. Border's eyes started flickering from left to right. 'Yeeesss.'

I noted his anxiety and explained how I'd stayed with a family who lived next door to him, but we never got the conversation back on track. The damage had been done. I loved the game too much and now I'd scared it away.

Boarding school

I 'checked in' to the Brisbane Grammar boarding house in June 1986. I was in Year 9 and my mid-term arrival was thanks to a vacancy at the school. Straightaway I could tell the place had a menacing vibe. A kid led me down the stairs, past threatening looks from fellow boarders wearing rugby jerseys, jeans and boat shoes, and into the Year 9 dormitory.

As I carried my case through the rows of beds, I overheard a conversation.

Schoolboy One: 'Nah, Harry doesn't have the biggest dick in the house, Fox does.'

Schoolboy Two: 'Bullshit, Harry does.'

Schoolboy One: 'Limp maybe, but Fox's is the biggest erect.'

That was concerning. I wondered how they all had detailed knowledge of each other's dicks. And then I saw the prison-style showers, where you were forced to wash yourself in front of boys sitting on a bench, waiting to take your place. I soon learned that if you turned the other way and showered with your bum facing the bench, you were viewed as someone ashamed of his dick and ridiculed. So you had to face outwards. Within a week, I knew what every boy in my dorm's dick looked like. I still do.

Max Howell was the headmaster of Brisbane Grammar School. Max was hulking and hunchbacked with thick Brylcreemed grey hair that stunk of cigars. During class breaks, he'd stand in the middle of the quadrangle as boys travelled from building to building, and if you got close enough to him, you had to say 'hello'. That's what I'd been told. 'Always say "hello" to Max. He won't say "hello" back, but make sure you say "hello" to him.' I'd only been there a few days when I passed Max in the quadrangle. As I walked by him, I looked at his face. It was a face deep in thunderous thought. It was a face that wanted to be left alone. So I put my head down and nearly made it past him before I heard, 'ZWAR!' I'd never heard our family name said like that, like a gunshot. So I immediately turned around, and as I was saying 'Yes', the back of his hand crashed into my face. I felt a thud, a ringing in my ears and the braces on my teeth embed themselves into my inner mouth. But I didn't cry.

He looked at me almost calmly, as if the act of backhanding me had sated him, and quietly told me to do my top button up as I was a disgrace. 'And when I address you, it's "Yes, Sir". Or "Yes, Mr Howell",' he said. 'Now get to class.'

I knew not to tell my parents about this. On the day I'd arrived, I'd heard cautionary tales of kids telling their parents about prefects or housemasters or Max beating up on them, which inadvertently made them bigger targets. It was clear: you either stayed and worked within the system, or you left.

I couldn't leave. Mum and Dad were so proud of me going to Brisbane Grammar. It made them feel like they were doing everything they could for my education. And that was kind of true. There were great mentors in the day school, like the cross-country coach, Mr Green, and my drama teacher, Mr Henderson. These were decent, smart, self-realised men who encouraged you to reach your potential. And the day students were also inspirations. Most were academically gifted and weren't about to allow

200 unruly boarders get in the way of their pursuit of excellence.

I'd probably been there about a month when I learned the boarding house was controlled by an internal organisation called 'the wanking police'. The wanking police were four self-appointed, popular kids who'd climb over the cubicle walls while you were on the toilet to make sure you weren't wanking. If you *were* wanking, then a complete shaming awaited. You might as well pack up and get yourself out of there because the way you were about to be treated would affect you for the rest of your life.

How it would go down is you'd be on the toilet, enjoying the only privacy on offer in that communal hellhole, when a surfy-looking dude would jump up onto the divider to check if you were wanking. If you weren't wanking, a disappointed look would fall across his brattish face and he'd hang there for a while, chatting away, until you reminded him you were in the middle of a poo. But if he saw you having a wank, he'd immediately scream, 'Garry Baker. Busted. Wanking.' Then he'd run from dorm to dorm like a medieval town crier, yelling, 'Garry Baker. Busted. Wanking,' and the whole boarding house would lose its mind. Word of the event would soon leak to the housemasters, who would lose their minds. And then the matron would find out – and she'd lose her mind. Then news of it would travel to the day school ... and that's where it would hit a roadblock. The day school produced three High Court justices, the author David Malouf, Robert Forster from the Go-Betweens and Brad Shepherd from the Hoodoo Gurus. These people were too urbane and socially aware to think there was anything weird about masturbation. They would look at the wanking police with the derision of 1500 David Gowers and say, 'Ha! Boarders!' then go back to arguing about the merits of Joy Division versus New Order.

But that didn't deter the boarders. They remained 100 per cent committed to the wanking police and that was never more obvious than on movie nights, when we'd all file into the assembly hall and watch a video that the duty prefect had selected to suit his tastes alone. On my first movie night, I tentatively made my way into the hall and sat next to the kids with the least aggressive body language. By the time the hall was about three-quarters full, a skinny kid with wavy hair and a protruding Adam's apple walked in. I would later find out that this was Tag O'Sullivan. As Tag looked for somewhere to sit, a low-level tribal chant broke out among the 150 boys assembled. It was terrifying and grew louder and louder. The words to the chant were: 'Tug-a-Tag-a-Tag-a-Tag-a-Tag, Tug-a-Tag-a-Tag-a-Tag-a-Tag, Tug-a-Tag-a-Tag-a-Tag-Tag ...' Tag had been caught wanking three years earlier.

They made that kid's life hell. The chant would always come out at assemblies. Sometimes it was enthusiastic; other times, it was casual. But the casual version was no less impactful. In fact, 200 boys *casually* chanting 'Tug-a-Tag-a-Tag-a-Tag' sometimes came across as more sinister than the enthusiastic version.

Returning to school after the Christmas break to begin Year 10, I'd barely made it into the reception area when I heard we had a new boy in our dorm and he'd already been busted. I took my luggage downstairs and saw a kid lying on his bed, facing the wall, his whole body shaking as he sobbed. I sat down next to him until he recovered enough to turn to me and say, 'What the fuck is going on?' I told him that they really don't like wanking here. And because I had no ability as a mental health professional, I invited him down the nets, where he revealed himself to be a capable left-arm spinner in the vein of Brad Hogg, skidding, with a little bit of turn. He said his name was Sam and he continued to sob as he bowled. He even sobbed as he gave me advice between deliveries. 'Make sure (sob) you get your front foot (sob) to the pitch of the ball (sob) and smother the spi-ii-innn (sob, sob).'

When Sam was 'busted' by the wanking police, he'd apparently told them that 'it was only natural'. From that moment on, whenever he walked into the assembly hall for Friday night films, 200 boys would yell in unison, 'It's ONLY natural. It's ONLY natural.' Did that mean a reprieve for Tag? No. Like Sam, Tug-a-Tag continued to be humiliated till his final day.

The most sinister element of the school was Skippy Lynch, the school's student counsellor. It was Skippy's job to help students if they were having general life difficulties, or their marks weren't living up to the score on the IQ test they were given when they first arrived at the school. His real name was Kevin, but we called him 'Skippy' because he'd suffered polio as a kid and instead of walking, he skipped in a sort of lumbering slow motion. Every three or four weeks, one of the boarders would go and see Skippy about his problems and return with a confused look on his face.

AZ: 'You OK, mate?'

Schoolboy One: 'I went in to see Skippy today ... and ... he cupped my balls.'

AZ: 'What?'

Schoolboy One: 'Yeah, I told him I'd been feeling a bit stressed and he stuck his hands down my pants and cupped my balls. Said it'd relax me.'

AZ: 'Did it relax you?'

Schoolboy One (confused): 'I dunno.'

Schoolboy Two: 'Yeah, when I'm stressed out, Skippy cups my balls too.'

AZ: 'Skippy never cups my balls.'

Schoolboy Two: 'No one wants to cup your balls, Zwar. Ha ha.'

Skippy sexually abused countless students. He died by suicide in 1997, aged 64, a day after he was charged with indecent dealing.

During the Royal Commission into Institutional Responses to Child Sexual Abuse, a survivor described how Max Howell walked into Lynch's office while he was being abused by Lynch. And Max Howell did nothing about it.

'Howell came into Lynch's office during one of our sessions and he saw me with my pants off and launched into a tirade about me being a sick individual or words to that effect,' the survivor told the commission. 'He asked me what was wrong with me. He got really angry and he told me to get out of here and go back to class. I left the room but Howell stayed behind and spoke to Lynch.'

Since 2000, Brisbane Grammar has reached agreements with 72 men who were abused by Lynch. And Max Howell's name has been removed from the MA Howell Indoor Sports Centre.

The lead-up to 1987

Before Border was captain, a succession of events in 1984 and 1985 set Australian cricket back on its heels. First, Greg Chappell, Lillee and Marsh retired. Then we played two series in a row against the all-conquering West Indies, which crushed our rebuilding team. There was the five-Test series in the West Indies, which we lost 3–nil. In the return series in Australia a few months later, we lost the First Test in Perth and the Second Test in Brisbane before Kim Hughes resigned as captain.

Hughes' batting form had collapsed under West Indian pace, and he was taking on a flood of criticism from former players and the media. When he read his resignation speech at a press conference in Brisbane, he cried. It was the first time I'd seen an adult male cry.

It was at this point that Allan Border got the top job. And it was a job he didn't necessarily want. He'd seen what it had done to Hughes and thought it was all a bit 'unsavoury'. Also, the role of captain had changed in the 1980s. As Chappell found, it wasn't just about playing and organising, it was also about coaching. The Australian Cricket Board rejected the idea of employing an actual coach because the prevailing wisdom was that coaches were for kids. Ian Chappell was particularly vocal about how unnecessary the position was and said that senior players should be able to hand out advice if and when needed. His brother Greg disagreed. He first pitched the idea of Australia having a coach to the Australian Cricket Board in 1980. Then Kim Hughes reintroduced the concept after Australia's disastrous World Cup in 1983. But Australia would have to sink lower before the role was given any serious consideration.

After Hughes resigned as captain, we limped through the rest of the 1984–85 series against the West Indies, losing 3–1. And when selectors announced the squad to tour England in 1985, Hughes wasn't in it. The former captain accused Australian cricket of not repaying his years of loyal service and called a press conference to announce he'd be leading an 'unofficial' tour of South Africa alongside Steve Rixon, Terry Alderman, John Dyson, Rodney Hogg and Carl Rackemann, who had all been selected for the Ashes tour. Each player would receive $200,000 tax-free Australian dollars, paid by the South African Federation. At the time, tours of South Africa were known as 'rebel tours' as the International Cricket Council had banned teams touring the country due to its government's policy of racial segregation, known as apartheid. Each of the 'rebels' would be disqualified from playing international cricket for three years and the then prime minister, Bob Hawke, would call them 'traitors'. For Border, this meant taking an even younger and more inexperienced side to England for the 1985 Ashes, which we lost 3–1.

When Australia lost the First Test to New Zealand in Brisbane at the start of the 1985–86 summer, it was clear Border was getting to the end of his rope. He'd scored 152 not out in eight defiant hours at the crease and was congratulated by a reporter in a post-match press conference. 'Big deal,' he said, pointing out that Australia had lost the Test by an innings. 'I just don't know what to do with these blokes anymore.' Australia would lose a series to New Zealand for the first time at home, 2–1.

Border's mood worsened when Australia travelled to New Zealand for the return series a few months later, losing 1–nil. On that tour, former Australian captain Bob Simpson had been given the role of 'assistant manager', but he was essentially there in an observational capacity to see how the Australian team was being run and whether it could benefit from a coach. Simpson said he was 'disgusted' by the Australian set-up, reporting his findings back to the Australian Cricket Board. However, the emergency button for getting Border help wasn't pressed until 21 March 1986, when the team arrived in Christchurch for a one-dayer and Border publicly lost his patience with the team he'd been carrying. Since being appointed captain, he'd made 1648 runs at 58.86 with six 100s and four 50s, but had won only three of 18 Tests. With journalists intercepting him on the way to a pre-match game of golf, Border cut loose, telling them his teammates were 'going to have to show me whether they really want to play for Australia and whether they really want to play under me'. He continued: 'From a personal point of view, I've achieved everything I've wanted to do. I've played in every country, got plenty of runs, hundreds against all countries. I don't need to keep going if it's no longer a pleasure. There are other things to consider. I have a wife and two young children I barely see. It's about time I considered them.'

That impromptu presser was the push the hierarchy of Australian cricket needed. What other options did they have? Losing Border was unthinkable.

Simpson took on the coaching gig, and the first thing to improve in the 1986–87 Ashes series was our fielding. But we still kept losing. After the Fourth Test in Melbourne, there was a rogue NSW-led coup to make Dirk Wellham captain for the final rubber in Sydney. Wellham wasn't even in the team, but Australian cricket had reached such a level of desperation, everything was on the table. We were down 2–nil in the Ashes and it had been 14 Tests since Australia had last won. But Border kept his job, Greg Matthews went to 12th man, and a little-known debutant, Peter Taylor, spun Australia to victory with eight wickets.

Still, no one was expecting big things from Australia in the '87 World Cup in India. Border's men had lost their previous five One Day Internationals and the odds of them taking home the Cup were a generous 16–1. Pakistani great Zaheer Abbas likened Australia to 'schoolboys' while *The Independent*'s acerbic Martin Johnson wrote that the Aussies 'couldn't beat a drum'. What they didn't know was Simpson had started to train his young side hard. So when Australia arrived in Chennai for its first game, no team was fitter or better drilled.

Boarding school part 2

The major bully in the boarding house was 'Rino' Patrick. He was over 6'4" and looked like Andre the Giant's less attractive brother. He had a pimple on the back of his neck that never went away. Sometimes the pimple would be covered by a bandaid, other times it was uncovered, proudly oozing in full view. Rino was in the first IV (tennis) and the first XI (cricket) and was not academically gifted, but teachers did no more than tut-tut at his lack of interest in his studies because they knew how important he was to the school's sporting success. When everyone else's English essays were about *Gatsby* or *Mockingbird*, Rino was allowed to pass his critical eye over Max Walker's *How to Hypnotise Chooks and Other Great Yarns*.

Rino also had slaves. His main slave was a kid we called 'Pancake' because he kept turning the ball over in games of footy. At night, we'd all be quietly doing our homework when a single clap would ring out. A single clap from Rino meant Pancake would have to drop and do 20 push-ups. Two claps meant Pancake would have to exit the boarding house at night, which was against the rules, and run two laps of the oval. Rino would often use his other slaves to hold kids he didn't like on the ground while he dropped his pants and placed his anus on the kid's nose. Rino called this 'choc nosing'. Once, Rino ate his own excrement as a joke, but the joke was on him because he ended up in the sick bay for two weeks, missing out on his cricket commitments and infuriating Max Howell. The boarders decided that reporting the incident to the day school wouldn't reflect well on us as a group. So when the 'day boys' asked us why Rino wasn't playing cricket, we could legitimately say he had the shits and leave it at that.

When Rino was in charge of our dormitory, he would regularly call Full Uniforms. A 'Full Uniform' was a punishment handed down late at night and involved all 30 members of a particular dormitory standing at the end of their beds in full uniform while the dorm prefect inspected their personal space and attire. If it wasn't up to scratch, the prefect would hit the boarder, and the boarder would not be able to retaliate. If the boarder did retaliate, the prefect would hand out a detention or bring down a bunch of his Year 12 mates to pummel the boarder. Fighting back just wasn't worth it. The prefect would take pot shots at us and we'd just have to wear them.

Normally, Full Uniforms were enforced after widespread misbehaviour in the dorm. In Rino's dorm, a Full Uniform could be called for any reason and no reason, and it didn't matter if we were all impeccably dressed and our areas spotless, Rino would beat the shit out of us anyway. The punishment that gave him the most satisfaction was a swinging elbow delivered to the area on the shoulder where the ligaments hold the bones together. When his elbow landed in the right spot, you'd feel an electric shock all through your body and not be able to move your arm. It was difficult to land the swinging elbow perfectly every time, but Rino had a pretty good strike rate. One after another, he left fifteen-year-old boys writhing in agony on their beds as he smilingly moved on to his next victim. When he got to me, Rino carefully rested his elbow on the spot he intended to hit. Then his elbow swung back before landing on my shoulder with a violent thud. It hurt, but I could still feel my arm, and Rino could see that I could still feel it. So he had another go ... and another. My shoulder was bruising heavily, but I wasn't in the same pain as the other guys. Rino was getting frustrated, so the next time he hit me, I 'acted' as though he'd hit the right spot and collapsed in the way I'd seen the others collapse, falling back on the bed and leaving the arm he hit completely limp.

Rino looked at me for a few beats – then smiled. Did I mention he had a silver tooth? 'Get up,' he said. I thought he'd bought my performance, so was careful to leave my right arm limp as I got up. He delivered a quick uppercut to my stomach. 'Don't bullshit me again,' he said. It took two or three more attempts for him to land his elbow in the right place, resulting in an electric shock, and rendering my arm useless with a dull, aching feeling that was exacerbated every time I tried to move.

When you look on the Brisbane Grammar School website today, there is a whole section devoted to 'Student Wellbeing' with its mission statement to nurture, care and encourage each member of the school's community. And the school has followed through on this. I went back to Grammar to give a speech in 2013 and the kids seemed unburdened and fearless. Same with the teachers. The cloud that had hovered over us in the late 80s had disappeared. In the headmaster's office, encased in a glass cabinet, sat Max Howell's cane. It served as a reminder of the school's brutal past, and to ensure it was never repeated.

1987 World Cup, India

The 1987 World Cup was the happiest time I experienced at boarding school. Maybe it was because I could just plug in headphones and escape the shit show. People go on about how '87 is the forgotten World Cup, but I remember everything about it. I remember the team was young; only Border and Peter Taylor were over 30. I remember reading about Tom Moody's mum secretly packing sweets, biscuits and Vegemite in the various compartments of his suitcase and how it kept Moody and his roommate, Steve Waugh, in good spirits. I remember being awed by the language of commentators Henry Blofeld and Christopher Martin-Jenkins. I hadn't known sports commentary could be poetic. But most importantly, I remember Simon O'Donnell wasn't well and that on the eve of the team leaving for India, he was given cortisone for lumps on his ribs. O'Donnell said he could tell his doctor was worried when he looked at X-rays of his ribs, but he still managed to get on the plane three days later. He didn't want to miss the World Cup and was prepared to play through pain and risk his condition becoming more serious. Two days into Australia's World Cup campaign, the lumps on O'Donnell's ribs returned, but he didn't say anything to his teammates or even the team doctor, worried that he'd be on the next plane home.

I liked O'Donnell. He was an Aquarius whose favourite meal was steak. He liked pop music – 'but not too loud' – and his greatest fear was growing old. O'Donnell had chosen to play cricket for Australia over football for St Kilda and since he'd sacrificed a potentially stellar career in AFL, I felt it incumbent on me to support him in any way I could.

Australia batted first in Game One against India in Chennai. It was the day Geoff Marsh established what would become known as 'the sheet anchor' role, where a batter holds up an end, playing a measured and riskless innings throughout the 50 overs, while his teammates hit out. Marsh scored a solid 110 in Australia's 270, a massive total helped along by David Boon's 49 off 68 balls and Dean Jones's 39 off 35. In fact, 270 would be equivalent to 350 these days. But India weren't intimidated and confidently set about mowing the score down. Border decided to bowl out spearheads Bruce Reid and McDermott early to try to keep Australia in the game after India's top three had brought the target within reach. That meant he needed someone else to bowl the final over, with India requiring six runs to win with one wicket in hand.

He chose the all-rounder Steve Waugh, who was inexperienced in bowling at the death, but had the cool head the occasion demanded. India's number 11, Maninder Singh, scored four runs off the first four balls of Waugh's over. It looked like India was going to win, only requiring two runs off two deliveries. Waugh was inscrutable. If his heart was racing, he didn't show it. With his fifth delivery, Waugh pulled out the slower ball. Singh completely mistimed it and was bowled. Australia won by a run ... and the legend of the final-over Ice Man was born.

Australia was a relentlessly fit team at the '87 World Cup. Simpson said the best fielding team would win the tournament, so they performed fielding drills on the lawns of every hotel they stayed in. In dispatches afterwards, it was the first time I'd heard the term 'soft-cockery' – coined by the Australian team's physiotherapist, Errol Alcott, while he was helping out in a fielding drill. The players complained Alcott was hitting balls too hard at them and Alcott responded that there was no room for 'soft-cockery', and the team would need to be a wimp-free zone if it were to win the World Cup. Soon, 'no soft-cockery' became part of the team ethos and Australia won five out of six matches before finding itself playing in the semifinal against Pakistan in Lahore. No Australian one-day team had ever won in Pakistan and it was hard to imagine them beating a team blessed with batting masters Javed Miandad and Saleem Malik, all-rounder Imran Khan, yorker specialist Wasim Akram, and the flamboyantly unplayable leg-spinner Abdul Qadir.

The Lahore crowd was fiercely partisan. Cheers for the home side's successes were deafening, whereas if the Australians did anything worthwhile, it was as though the whole stadium had been put on mute.

Border won the toss and batted. David Boon (65), Geoff Marsh (31) and Dean Jones (38) were solid at the top, but it was newcomer Mike Veletta's 48 from 50 and Steve Waugh's 18 off the final over that helped us get to 267. Pakistan responded well with Miandad (70) and Imran (58) giving the home side a sniff of victory. Then Craig McDermott's shattering 5–44 ensured the home side fell 18 runs short and Australia booked its first World Cup final. But Border's men were forced to curtail their celebrations when officials noted a growing hostility in the stands and organised them to be evacuated from the stadium and sent on a private plane to Kolkata for the final against England.

The thrill of victory was tempered by Simon O'Donnell's deteriorating condition. He had bowled beautifully throughout the tournament, deceiving batsmen with a combination of medium pacers and change-up leg spinners. Australia couldn't afford to lose him, even though he was in excruciating pain and couldn't even muster the energy for the team song which he usually led after every Australian win. Dean Jones said O'Donnell knew something was wrong – 'Really wrong'. But after a conversation with coach Bob Simpson, he decided to play in the final.

In front of an overflowing crowd at Eden Gardens, Kolkata, Border won the toss and batted. Boon (75), Marsh (24) and Jones (33) ensured our innings was well set-up, but we weren't scoring quickly enough, so Border sent in McDermott as a pinch-hitter. The big Queenslander did his job with 14 from 8. Then Veletta's 45 from 31 deliveries helped us to a competitive 5–253.

England's start wasn't flawless, with McDermott removing opener Tim Robinson for 0 and O'Donnell taking the prized scalp of Graham Gooch for 35. But then Bill Athey and Mike Gatting put on 69 runs and had the chase well under control at 2–135 after 31 overs. And that's when Gatting inexplicably tried to reverse-sweep Border. The esteemed cricket periodical *Wisden* would later call the shot 'too crass to contemplate'. What made it worse was that if the England skipper had let the ball go, it would have been a rank leg-side wide. But an overly confident Gatting took the cute approach and paddled the ball straight into the gloves of wicketkeeper Greg Dyer. It turned out most of my dormitory was listening to the match on their headphones, because we all cheered at the same time.

Worryingly, Allan Lamb (45) and Phil DeFreitas (17) weren't giving up and they kept the boundaries flowing. With two overs to go, England needed 20 to win. But once Steve Waugh removed DeFreitas, there was no way Neil Foster and Gladstone Small were going to get the runs. Australia won by 8. In two years, we'd gone from Bob Simpson calling us a 'disgrace' to the champions of the world. Reports at the time were that Australia's celebrations were subdued. The team was more exhausted than elated. But most Australians weren't able to judge the situation for themselves because cricket broadcast rights holders Channel Nine didn't telecast the moment in Brisbane, Sydney or Melbourne. Maybe they thought no one would watch, or that Australia wouldn't win. In fact, they didn't broadcast 99 per cent of the tournament. When Australia won its first game against India, Nine screened *The Man from Snowy River.* When Australia won the semifinal in Pakistan, Nine screened *Romancing the Stone.* However, Nine *did* show the first innings of the final in most of the country. But for the second innings – when Gatting was reverse-sweeping and Border was lifting Australia's first World Cup trophy – Nine screened *Unfaithfully Yours*, starring Dudley Moore and Nastassja Kinski. In Adelaide, the programming was more cricket-friendly, with Nine screening the whole first innings and most of the second, and viewers were able to see McDermott's final over and former England skipper-turned-commentator Tony Lewis saying, 'And listen to the acclaim. To be cheered by 90,000 spectators at Eden Gardens, Kolkata, and take your first World Cup. That is Australia's joy and England's misery.' The only South Australian viewers not delighted by the scenes from Eden Gardens were English expats and those who had tuned in hoping to see the advertised program, which was *The Natural*, starring Robert Redford and Glenn Close.

Still, radio was good enough for the kids in my dorm. The whistles and yells went on for several minutes as the relentlessly professional Blofeld and Martin-Jenkins revealed no disappointment as they described Australia's celebrations.

A day after the all-conquering team returned home, O'Donnell went straight to hospital, where he was diagnosed with non-Hodgkin's lymphoma and operated on to remove parts of his ribs. He said he was 'frightened. Very frightened.' But after three months of chemotherapy, the 24-year-old was cancer-free.

'You live with [cancer] every day,' O'Donnell told the *Herald Sun* in 2012. 'I thought about it this morning, having a shower. You check, you monitor how you feel, that's just the life you live now.'

CHAPTER 3

The 1992 World Cup and Goodbye to Border

'I don't ask Kathy to face Michael Holding, so there's no reason why I should be changing nappies.'

– Ian Botham on marriage and parenting

After the '87 World Cup, the next big turning point for the Border–Bob Simpson show was the 1989 Ashes tour of England. Again, no one gave Border's team a chance. But Border had played County cricket for Essex during the previous season and seen two out-of-favour Australians thriving in English conditions, so he ensured they had a seat on the plane. The first was 33-year-old Terry Alderman, who was coming to the end of his career and had never really reached the potential he showed in the '81 Ashes, when he'd taken 42 wickets. Border had watched Alderman trap Graham Gooch LBW during a County game and decided that the medium pacer was born to bowl in England. The other was Steve Waugh, who'd averaged 30 after 26 Tests, and was still without a Test century to his name. But that summer, Waugh had scored eight centuries for Somerset, and Border knew he'd be a vital part of the Australian set-up. Both players went on to perform exceptionally in the Ashes, Alderman taking 41 wickets and Waugh averaging 126. Newcomer Mark Taylor was also a revelation, making 839 runs at 83.90.

The other tactic Border had up his sleeve was to be deliberately taciturn whenever the England team tried to interact with him. In the 1985 and 1986–87 Ashes series, he'd got on famously with England captain David Gower and the teams had been social. But Border wanted to stamp out the notion that Australia was England's easygoing little brother, happy to lose and then have a beer. So after the toss before the First Test in '89, Gower was wrong-footed when he tried to make conversation with Border and got donuts. 'In '85, we talked all the time,' said Gower. 'But in '89, I only heard him say "heads" or "tails" until about August.'

'I made a personal choice to have a harder edge as captain, be more stand-offish towards [England],' Border said after the tour. 'It was a hard thing to do and they all got the shits, but it was all part and parcel of what I wanted to achieve.'

Australia would win the '89 Ashes 4–nil. The seeds planted in that series would bear fruit over the coming decades. More immediately, the darkest era in Australian cricket history was over and Border's men started winning regularly. They beat Pakistan, Sri Lanka, and England 3–nil in the return Ashes series. Sure, they lost 2–1 on a tour of the West Indies, but the gap between the sides was closing. Then came the marathon 1991–92 summer. First up was the five-test series against India, which we won 4–nil, and was also notable for Shane Warne's debut. Warne played in the Third and Fourth Tests, then was dropped for the Fifth in Perth. His overall figures for the series were 1 for 228 and gave no indication of what was to come. Australia went straight from the Test series into the World Series Cup against India and the West Indies, winning seven of the ten matches. By the time the World Cup started on 22 February 1992, I wondered if Border's team might just be a bit exhausted. Maybe it was because I was exhausted watching them. The summer had already been a full meal. But I still thought they'd win. We were the reigning champions and runaway favourites.

The Australians' first match was against New Zealand at Eden Park, Auckland, on a low, slow, clay-based flat pitch. New Zealand batted first and made 248, which was probably par. Australia's response was immediately thrown off-balance by Kiwi captain Martin Crowe's decision to open the bowling with off spinner Dipak Patel – a new tactic in those days – before following up with a bunch of part-time medium pacers. The result was that the ball didn't come onto the bat and we were put off our game. Two run-outs didn't help either. Australia would lose by 37 runs despite a stoic century from David Boon.

In Sydney against the South Africans, we made a miserable 9 for 170, and they lost only one wicket in chasing down our total. It felt like a betrayal to see former Australian opener turned South African captain Kepler Wessels making 81 against us and being awarded man of the match. Australia won by a single run against India, thanks to 90 from Dean Jones. But when we batted first against England, we were all out for 171 after Ian Botham tore through us, taking four wickets. Then openers Botham and Gooch set up an easy win for the English. We won handsomely against Sri Lanka before coming up against an out-of-form Pakistan in Perth. Imran Khan's side had lost to the West Indies, won against Zimbabwe, had an abandoned match against England, lost to India, and then lost again to South Africa. They were on three points after five matches, compared to Australia's four. Both teams needed to win this match to keep their World Cup chances alive. I tried to convince myself that Australia had been foxing and this was the day we were finally going to get serious. But I was wrong. It was the day *Imran* decided to get serious.

The Oxford University–educated all-rounder had come out of retirement for the World Cup so he could raise money to build a cancer hospital in Lahore. The hospital would be in memory of his mother, who had been unable to get treatment in Pakistan and died of cancer in 1986. Most of his match fees went to the hospital, as did proceeds from charity dinners and man-of-the-match cars, which he'd auction off. But if Imran and Pakistan were to make any money out of this World Cup, they had to start winning.

When Imran arrived for Pakistan's pre-match training session in Perth, he wore a T-shirt with a tiger emblazoned on it. He proceeded to give his men a speech for the ages. As journalist Osman Samiuddin would write in his essay 'The Miracle of '92', Imran told every player to look inside themselves and understand how great they were. 'You,' he asked one, 'is there a more talented player in the world than you?' Then he pointed individually to each of the other players. 'Is there a better fielder than you? Or a better batsman than you?' Imran then invoked the image on his shirt. 'Fight like cornered tigers, because nothing is more dangerous than a cornered tiger.' It worked. Pakistan made 220 and all we could muster in return was another score in the 170s. We were hammered. It was a humiliating defeat.

To make the semifinals, Australia would have to win their final two matches and hope Pakistan would lose one of theirs. Although we racked up wins against Zimbabwe and the West Indies, when Pakistan beat Sri Lanka and New Zealand, it was over. Pakistan had edged us out of the semifinals, courtesy of the point it picked up from a rain-abandoned match against

England. I remember being in front of the television, nestled in a beanbag, when I found out we wouldn't be playing in the semis. There's nothing sadder than a sad man in a beanbag.

It's hard to work out what went wrong. Steve Waugh says the team lacked 'hustle and energy'. Opener Geoff Marsh scoring slowly and stoically up one end didn't work anymore. Teams were now using pinch-hitters to open the batting so they could make the most of fielding restrictions in the first 15 overs. Australia tried to fix its situation on the fly, playing eight games with five different opening combinations. We started with Marsh and David Boon, then moved on to Mark Taylor and Marsh with Boon at three, then Tom Moody and Taylor, then Moody and Marsh, before settling on Moody and Boon for the final two matches.

After Pakistan's win against Australia, it kept on winning all the way to the World Cup final against England in Melbourne. The only Aussie to make an impact on that game was comedian Gerry Connolly, who offended the English playing group with his impersonation of the Queen at the official pre-match function. Connolly, performing in front of both teams, officials and sponsors, had barely started his act when Ian Botham and Graham Gooch downed their cutlery and left the room. Connolly was perplexed. 'I wasn't murdering babies.'

Botham felt he had every reason to be upset, and probably still does. When he was interviewed about it

15 years later, he said he had no regrets about leaving the dinner. 'I'm there and some poofter gay guy comes on stage in drag with a stuffed corgi under his arm and takes the piss out of the Queen,' Botham told UK sports history website sportsasylum.co.uk. 'Why should I put up with that?'

On the day of the final, Pakistan made 249 batting first, Imran Khan starring with an elegant 72. Gooch and Botham opened for England and put on six runs together before Botham fell to Wasim Akram. The rest of the team didn't fare much better, with England all out for 227.

After the match, Imran donated his entire World Cup earnings to his cancer hospital, which would finally open two years later. Today, 75 per cent of patients at the hospital are treated for free.

The 1992 World Cup remains an unpleasant memory for everyone involved in the Australian team. They were thrown off balance against New Zealand and weren't able to right themselves till the end. Australian officials also learned the hard way not to burn out their team with a bunch of meaningless matches before such a big tournament. All these lessons were heeded in 2015, when we hosted the Cup again and finally got it right.

Years after the tournament, journalist Daniel Brettig interviewed Ian Healy about the keeper's penchant for collecting the different uniforms from his many series and tours. When asked if he'd kept his

1992 World Cup shirt, Healy looked in his wardrobe and couldn't find it.

'It shows how little I wanted to remember it,' he said.

USQ

It was important to me to get as far away from Grammar people as possible, which meant not going to the University of Queensland, where many of my former schoolmates attended lectures in their school rugby jerseys. So I went to the University of Southern Queensland in Toowoomba. It had only recently taken that name. A couple of years before, it had been called the Darling Downs Institute of Advanced Education, or the DDIAE. There had been a jingle on television designed to lure students to the college: '*If you wanna degree, go to D-D-I-A-E.*'

I wanted a degree, but I wanted a degree in acting. Dad was concerned about the employment opportunities in acting and suggested I do something that might actually lead to a job. So I enrolled in journalism and moved into campus accommodation. It was an exciting time because, unlike Grammar, everyone was pleasant and relaxed. It took me a while to deprogram myself and shed the hang-ups of being institutionalised. I made great friends, all of whom had gone to state schools. I didn't hide where I'd gone to school, but didn't broadcast it either. It just wasn't the type of information that would make any conversation better. But a private school education did come in handy at formal occasions when my friends would ask me to tie their ties for them. It was strange that the idea of being useful – if only for a few moments – somehow made all the beatings worthwhile.

Toward the end of the year, I met Hayley while competing in a theatre sports competition. She was smart, funny, had dirty-blonde hair and smoked, but it was hard to get a handle on her because she didn't seem 100 per cent present in the relationship. Then again, I'd never been in a relationship before, so I didn't know how 'present' you were meant to be. All I knew was that her coldness made me like her more. When it came time for the Christmas break, I returned to Cairns and she returned to her home town on the Sunshine Coast. I called her a few times, but she never called me. I was new to relationships, so made a million excuses as to why she couldn't pick up the phone. When we reconvened in the new year, it turned out Hayley had spent the summer with her ex-boyfriend. I thought that was the end of our relationship, but Hayley explained she was living proof you could be in love with two people at the same time. I wasn't delighted with the new arrangement, but hung around in the hope there'd be a change in the weather. And there was. After a month of me being her boyfriend during the week and her ex being her boyfriend at weekends, she said she was now only in love with one person, and it wasn't me. I was devastated. I visited her off-campus share house to confirm our relationship was absolutely over. She said it was. And even though I tried to respond like John Cusack in *Grosse Pointe Blank*, I think what came out was closer to John Cusack in *Say Anything*. My eyes behaved as if I'd been told I had 15 minutes to live. And to pile on the insults, I was attacked by a magpie on my way back to campus.

I didn't see Hayley for several weeks after that. It wasn't like I spent the time crying but, like 'Big' from *Sex and the City*, I did listen to a lot of Sinatra. Then, on a typically windy and chilly Toowoomba night, two men walked into the college dining area where I was eating with 150 others and the whole place immediately fell silent. Everyone knew they were cops. No one else on campus wore Roger David. They strode over and told me to accompany them back to the station. It was there that I learned that Hayley's car had been stolen, and when the police asked her if there was anyone who might be upset with her, anyone who had a reason to be vengeful, she told them she'd recently broken up with me and I'd been pretty distraught about it. She said she didn't think I'd be the type to steal a car, but she couldn't rule it out. Well, that was good enough for Toowoomba's finest to give me the full *Blue Murder* treatment – yelling, followed by threats, followed by more yelling, followed by them walking out of the interview room and leaving me there by myself for half an hour, followed by them telling me they'd found the car *and* the thief and I was free to go back to college. And no, a taxi would not be provided for my convenience.

After that, heartbreak would hit me in waves as I went through the motions of getting my journalism degree, pining for the acting course, and writing for the university newspaper. Half of my contributions were think-pieces designed to be self-deprecatingly funny, but were interpreted by everyone who read them as a cry for help. The other half were theatre reviews of shows put on by the university's acting students. One of my early reviews was for a production of *Salome*, where an actor listed in the program as 'Jason W Gann' shone in the role of John the Baptist. Jason was extremely watchable and the only one on stage who made the arch dialogue seem real. In my glowing review of his performance, I purposefully referred to him as 'Jason Gann' and not 'Jason W Gann', because I thought the 'W' left him open to ridicule. A few days after the review appeared, Jason approached me in the quadrangle and said, 'Are you Adam Zwar?' I said I was and prepared to be thanked for the sparkling write-up. Instead, he said, 'It's Jason W Gann, mate.'

I said, 'I don't think the "W" works for you, mate.' He said he thought it did. And I said we'd have to agree to disagree.

At the end of second year, I successfully auditioned for the acting course and arranged with the university to do third-year journalism at the same time as first-year acting. It was a relief to be enrolled in the course I wanted to be doing all along. And for the first time in months, I started feeling confident about the direction of my life. I wasn't moping around anymore. I started socialising and getting involved in university activities. So when I was asked to take part in the annual slaughter that was the Arts versus Engineering game of rugby league, of course I said, 'Yes'.

The engineers kicked off. A visual arts major caught the ball, saw a pack of men with goatees bearing down on him and, with zero duty of care, threw the ball over his head. Foolishly, I caught the ball, and sold a few dummies before being gang tackled. My jersey was pulled over my head and my face was repeatedly punched. When I walked off the ground, my nose was rubber and my eyes were starting to close up.

I went to the doctor and she confirmed my nose was broken. Then she said, 'We can straighten it if you like ... but it's not as though you're ever going to be on television.' That hurt more than the broken nose. I nodded – I was certain she knew something I didn't.

Goodbye Mr Border

Allan Border was 37, approaching his tenth year as captain, and on his last lap of the cricket merry-go-round. There was just one goal left to achieve and that was to beat the West Indies in a series. Australia hadn't won a Test series against them for 17 years. It was the only mountain left to climb. The team headed into the Fourth Test in January 1993 one–nil up. They had drawn in Brisbane and Sydney and won in Melbourne after Shane Warne took a magnificent 7–52 in the Windies' second innings. The Fifth Test would be in Perth and Border knew Australia's chances of winning on a hard WACA wicket against fast bowlers Courtney Walsh and Curtly Ambrose were slim. So it was Adelaide or bust.

The West Indies made 252 in their first innings. Australia responded with 213, with 22-year-old debutant Justin Langer wearing multiple blows to the head and body from Walsh and Ian Bishop. The Windies capitulated to 146 in their second innings thanks to a mesmerising spell from hometown boy Tim May, who took five wickets in six overs. That left Australia 186 to win. Ambrose, Bishop and Walsh tore through the Aussies' second innings, with the only resistance in the top six coming from Langer, who made 54. So with nine down and 46 to win, Craig McDermott joined Tim May at the crease. May told the number 11 to not look at the scoreboard and play it 'ball by ball'. McDermott batted bravely and confidently and the runs started ticking over. The only way the batters knew they were getting closer to the required target was when the crowd's roar grew louder and louder with each run scored. Finally, with just two to win and one to tie, Walsh bowled a short one to McDermott, who turned his back on the ball at the last moment. There was a suspicious clipping noise as the ball made its way past McDermott and into keeper Junior Murray's gloves and the umpire immediately gave it out. The West Indies were exultant – Walsh running about 80 metres with his delirious teammates in pursuit.

In the commentary box, Greg Chappell said, 'I can't believe it.' Neither could Border. He'd been sitting in the same seat since he'd lost his wicket, per the Australian superstition of not moving from your seat once a partnership had developed so you don't break the spell. When the umpire's finger went up, Border hurled the cricket ball he'd been nervously clutching into the dressing room floor. To rub salt into gaping wounds, when the dismissal was replayed from the perspective of the camera behind the batter, it was clear the ball didn't go near McDermott's bat, but had shaved the visor on his helmet.

It was quiet in the dressing room. No one said a single word for 20 minutes. Players just stared at the ground. That's when federal Opposition Leader John Hewson walked in. Post-match dressing room invitations really should come with a caveat that you're invited to meet the players 'as long as they haven't just experienced a heartbreaking loss due to a howling umpiring error or similar'. When Hewson entered the room, he took in the mood and wisely didn't try to engage anyone in small talk. He just sat on a bench for quite a few minutes before the tension got the better of him.

'Well, did you hit it or not?' Hewson asked McDermott.

'No!' said McDermott.

That broke the ice. Players started talking, laughing and commiserating. Meanwhile, the party raged so hard in the West Indies dressing room that the South Australian Cricket Association had to bill the team for damage after what its management called an 'outpouring of emotion'.

The Windies did go on to win in Perth by an innings and 25 runs, taking home the Frank Worrell Trophy. Again.

That heartbreak aside, Border's farewell lap in 1993 included a successful Ashes tour, a series win against New Zealand at home, and a series draw against South Africa. In his last victorious Test, he scored 17 and 42 not out, which brought his run total for all Tests to 11,174.

And that was it. Was he as revered as Bradman? Maybe more so. Border wasn't a superman like Bradman. He was a human man who'd wrung every bit of potential out of his body for the love of country.

After Mum and Dad, he was the most important person in my life. I sweated on his every innings, and when he neared the end and his powers were ever so slightly waning, I crossed fingers and toes that his average would remain above 50. He retired with an average of 50.56.

After he walked off the oval in Durban in his last appearance for Australia, I tried and failed to imagine what it would be like to never again see his name at number five on the Australian card, or his stocky frame in a floppy hat at second slip, or his glorious direct hits from mid wicket, or his gentle left-arm tweaks which always picked up wickets but were only used when he'd run out of options. It was all over. To show our appreciation, we named a couple of cricket grounds and a medal after him. I'm sure he was delighted, but he deserved so much more. He was the Churchill of Australian cricket. The indomitable spirit who came to the fore when his country needed him most.

Every now and then when I need cheering up, I go to YouTube and watch footage from a 1993 Ashes tour match against Somerset where the 5'8" Border tells a recalcitrant 6'3" Craig McDermott to improve his attitude. The footage starts with Border trying to get the fast bowler's attention.

Border: 'Hey! Hey! Hey!'

McDermott: 'What'd I do?'

Border: 'I'm fuckin' talking to you, come here.'

McDermott: 'I'm right.'

Border: 'Come here. Come here. Come here.'

Then there's an edit in the video and we return with Border striding back to his fielding position.

Border: 'You fuckin' do that again mate, and you'll be on the next plane home.'

McDermott says something inaudible as Border's back is turned. Border hears it and swings his body toward McDermott, shoulders back and chest puffed out.

Border: 'What's that?'

McDermott: 'Nothing. I didn't say a thing.'

Border: 'You fuckin' test me, mate, we'll see.'

At that moment, Border was Australia's dad.

CHAPTER 4

Dean Jones and Australia A

'He was all bristle and bullshit and I couldn't make out what he was saying, except that every sledge ended with "arsewipe".'

– Mike Atherton on Merv Hughes

Dean Jones made his Test debut on the 1984 tour of the West Indies. It was a quiet entry with scores of 48, 5, 1 and 11. He was then dropped. Two years later, in 1986, he was selected to go to India and was rooming with a young Mike Veletta. Both men were in contention for the open number three spot for the First Test in Chennai, but it was Jones who got the call to visit the skipper in his room. Border gave Jones a lemonade, sat him at the end of his hotel room bed, and challenged Jones to make number three his own. That meant tempering his aggressive instincts and occupying the crease for long periods. As Jones left the room, Border told him, 'I believe in your ability.'

In his book *Cricket Beyond the Bazaar*, journalist Mike Coward says Jones was determined to prove his worth and repay Allan Border's faith in him. As he made his way to the middle in the 22nd over, he kept telling himself to play straight and conservatively. And he did. His first 50 came in three hours and 42 minutes. But with the temperature in the mid-40s and humidity over 80 per cent, Jones started to struggle with nausea from dehydration. He was on 87 when the heat and humidity finally got to him and he vomited ... for the first time.

When nightwatchman Ray Bright was dismissed for 30, he got back to the dressing room and suddenly found he couldn't breathe. A doctor was summoned as the left-arm spinner screamed, 'I can't get air. I can't get air.' Bright started to panic and had to be physically restrained by team physio Errol Alcott. As Bright slowly began breathing again, Jones kept batting. His first Test century came in five hours and 32 minutes. When he got to 150, his body started shutting down. He kept withdrawing to the side of the wicket between deliveries to vomit. When he wasn't vomiting, he was urinating in his flannels. Then he started getting cramps in his legs and stomach – yet his batting remained unaffected. When he got to 174, he told Border, who was batting with him, that he couldn't go on as his stomach was in his mouth. Famously, and unsympathetically, Border said, 'If that's the way you feel, let's get a real Australian out here. A Queenslander.' When this story is told, what is conveniently left out is that the 'real Australian' due to come in next was the not-so-fit Greg 'Fat Cat' Ritchie. But Border's goading worked, and Jones redoubled his efforts, making it to 200 in seven hours and 15 minutes.

At tea, he was 202 not out. Inside the dressing room, 12th man Dave Gilbert joined Australian squad members Simon Davis and Mike Veletta in stripping Jones's sodden clothes off him. They tried to cool and hydrate him before dressing and sending him out again, but this time they forgot to furnish him with a protector or thigh pad. He lasted 14 more minutes before being bowled. Somehow, he made it back to the dressing room and was placed in an ice bath.

Alcott noted that Jones was unable to control bladder function or stop vomiting, so he called an ambulance to take him to hospital; a small van turned up instead. Nevertheless, Jones was stretchered inside, drifting in and out of consciousness as he was driven through the back streets of Chennai to Apollo Hospital. As the van hurriedly took corners, Jones would be tipped from the stretcher, his body spasming. Alcott pleaded with the driver to slow down, but he wouldn't, so Alcott leaned on Jones to stop him from being dislodged again.

They arrived at the hospital, and five doctors competed to tend to the cricketing hero. Three bottles of saline later, Jones was feeling a little better – albeit four kilos lighter and with impaired speech and vision.

He would tell Mike Coward, 'I had to do something mentally tough to show I could play Test cricket. That is what AB had said. That was always in the back of my mind.'

Dean Jones would go on to score 11 Test centuries and average 46.5 in 52 Tests. He charged at the West Indian pace quartet while every other Australian was just trying to survive them, wore sunglasses before everyone else and slapped zinc cream onto his bottom lip. As a kid, I'd try to emulate how Jones nimbly danced down the wicket, but I couldn't concentrate on two things at once. So if I was concentrating on the dance, I wasn't concentrating on the ball, which often sailed right past me onto middle stump. I didn't even bother with the cover drive on one knee. I knew my limitations.

Jones made cricket unmissable. No one walked away from a television when he was at the crease. He dismantled bowling attacks that featured Wasim Akram, Waqar Younis and Richard Hadlee. He always found gaps, ran like an athlete and sometimes turned blind for the second, happily telling people how much time he saved in doing so. His batting was utterly compelling and worth every shiver he gave you as he scratched around at the start while getting his eye in.

Jones was the first fielder I saw slide toward the boundary feet first to collect the ball. These were the days before ropes were brought in to protect fielders, and he'd fearlessly slide into the advertising signs like a baseballer sliding onto a base. Mid-slide, he'd collect the ball and throw it back in one action. This is regulation now, but Jones did it first.

After 52 Tests, Jones had made many more runs than Ricky Ponting and Steve Waugh at the same point, and marginally more than Allan Border and Ian Chappell. But the selectors decided they'd had enough of him and we'll never really know why. Was he too outspoken? A show-off? A controversialist? Well, there was that time he wrote a column about how Australia had played with more freedom in a one-dayer against South Africa because coach Bob Simpson was away sick. Simpson was furious and threatened to sue Jones if he didn't apologise in print – which Jones immediately did. But that storm lasted less than a week and was hardly a sackable offence. We can only conclude that the selectors simply didn't like the cut of Jones's jib and that's why he was dumped from the Test line-up in September 1992 for the prodigious 21-year-old Damien Martyn. Jones fans were inconsolable. His last seven scores in Test cricket were 150, 10, 57, 77, 100, 11 and 21. Broadcaster Tim Lane called Jones's axing 'one of the most statistically contrary in Australian cricket history'.

Jones continued to play one-dayers for Australia until he was dropped from that side toward the end of an eight-game series against South Africa in April

1994. Australia was down 4–3 and needed to win the final match to square the series.

'Everything was on the line, and Mark Taylor [captain] and David Boon [vice-captain] picked themselves before me,' Jones said on Shane Watson's 'Lessons Learnt with the Greats' podcast. 'I said, "Are you trying to tell me that you're a better player than me, in one-day cricket? Really? Well, that's it, I'm done."' Jones retired from international cricket immediately and told Watson he quickly regretted the decision.

A few months later, the Australian Cricket Board was looking to add the element of a second XI Australian side to what promised to be a dour World Series Cup Tri-series between Australia, England and Zimbabwe. The second XI would be called Australia A. As the concept gained traction in the press, Jones – who'd been in cracking form in Shield cricket that summer, including scoring a triple century – put up his hand to captain the side. The selectors dead-batted the offer: as far as they were concerned, Jones had retired. It was an excuse that rang hollow. Jones called their bluff, saying that the ICC had ruled that Australia A wasn't an officially sanctioned international team 'so maybe I don't have to come out of retirement anyway'. The ball was in the selectors' court.

Every Jones fan held out hope for one more chance to see the magician in action – just one last dance down the wicket, slide into the boundary to rake in a runaway ball or glimpse of zinc on the bottom lip. But would the planets align?

Brisbane

I had graduated from my journalism degree at the University of Southern Queensland, but had been kicked out of its acting school. The whole acting course was an unpleasant experience from the moment our lecturer put images of the faces of everyone in our class on a projector, then used a program to divide each face in half to show us who in the class had a symmetrical face and who didn't. He explained that if you were to have a career in front of the camera, it was important to have a symmetrical face. There were some people in the class (female) whose projected faces he lingered on for an uncomfortable amount of time, detailing the evenness of their features like he was describing *Starry Night Over the Rhône*. Then he put my image up there. 'This,' he said, laughing, 'this is what an asymmetrical face looks like. This is a face for radio.' I waited to see if the class laughed at his hacky joke. They didn't; they were a good class. At the end of first semester second year, the lecturers kicked out actors who they didn't think were up to snuff. It was called 'the June prune'. One by one we sat in front of a panel of them and were told our fate. It turned out my fate didn't align with theirs. The official explanation was that

I'd failed movement, but I just think they didn't like the cut of my asymmetrical face. And that was it. Three and a half years in Toowoomba over. I loved the place. It was a post-boarding-school sanctuary. I found friends there and acceptance, probably for the first time in my life, and now it was over.

I moved back to Cairns and into my childhood bedroom which still had a Jeff Thomson poster hanging on the wall – the one where he sticks his tongue out at the point of delivery. Then I got a job washing dishes at a five-star hotel, which is exactly the same as washing dishes at a one-star hotel – except at the five-star hotel, dish pigs were called 'stewards'. We wore blue overalls and I was the only one in my team who hadn't done time. I desperately wanted to get out of Cairns and move to Brisbane or Melbourne, but what was I going to do there – get another dishwashing job? I wanted to be an actor but I had to park that dream and work with what I had, which was a journalism degree. Every day, I'd pore through the 'Situations Vacant' section in all the papers, hoping to see something that might suit a journalism graduate. I applied to QTV, *The Cairns Post*, *The Townsville Bulletin* and *The Courier-Mail*. There were no bites. Then I saw a little ad in *The Australian* for a rugby league writer at *The Sunday Telegraph* (Brisbane Edition) – Rupert's attempt to give Queensland another Sunday option – and I applied. The editor told me to watch the Broncos–Penrith game that Saturday afternoon and fax through a 1000-word match report five minutes after the siren. So I sat my Xerox word processor in front of the game and my hands became a blur as I typed up every try, penalty, conversion, punch-on and difference of opinion with the ref. I was all adrenalin, fuelled by the desire to no longer wash dishes with people who could make me disappear if I looked at them sideways. In this one moment, all the years of watching televised sport and then reading about it in detail the next day helped me get my first professional job.

Dad took me to the bus terminal for the 24-hour trip to Brisbane. I was nervous that I wouldn't fit in, but I'd grown up with journalists and knew how to at least act like one until I worked out how to be one. I shook Dad's hand and was about to grab my suitcases out of the back when he said he had something to tell me.

I nodded.

'Your mother's got breast cancer,' he said. 'Tomorrow, she's going to be getting a mastectomy.'

I couldn't think or speak or breathe. I was frightened. Dad's eyes were red and his breathing was shallow. It was the first time I'd seen him vulnerable. He was 40 when I was born, now he was 62. This seemed to be the first problem his sheer force of personality couldn't control. When I finally got enough air in my lungs to speak, I said I wouldn't go. But he told me it'd help Mum to know I was 'gainfully' employed.

'Hurry up,' he said, his eyes now glassy with tears. 'You're going to miss your bus.'

Mum was brought up by a single mother in Sydney. She had at least one stepfather, who I could tell she'd had a difficult relationship with. Maybe that was why she was sent off to live with her grandparents and then to boarding school. If I sound vague on her upbringing, it's because she rarely talked about it. You'd just hear non-linear snippets of her life and have to put it together yourself.

Her stories started when she went to London in her 20s. She was a nurse before putting herself through art school. When she met Dad, she was working in interior design. They'd only been on a few dates when Dad left London for a year to join Peter Thomson on the golf tour and write *This Wonderful World of Golf*. Mum and Dad must've known they'd be together forever because Dad said he'd take Mum's mother, Olive, out to lunch when he got to Sydney. Mum sent Olive one of those blue aerograms letting her know the arrangement and warning, 'You should know that Des is bald. I don't have a problem with it.'

Beyond being a wonderful writer and cook, Mum helped the ill, the sensitive, the grieving and the creatively talented but emotionally fraught. She'd seek them out and invite them around for dinner. She was also funny. She'd refer to herself as 'Sadie', as in the 'cleaning lady' protagonist in John Farnham's 1967 hit song. When she'd tell me about the latest restaurant opening she had been to, she'd say, 'Sadie got an airing last night.' Everyone knew their place in our house, and that place was the 1950s. And if a photo shoot for *House & Garden Magazine* was going overtime, her way of getting everyone to hurry up would be to say, 'Chop chop – Des and Adam will be waiting at the dinner table with their mouths open.'

I wasn't the only one worried about Mum. If anything happened to her, more than 100 people would be without their treasured confidante.

The first few weeks at *The Sunday Telegraph* passed in a haze as I awaited news on Mum's operation, then her treatment and recovery. Dad called every day, giving me reports. We were both in a state of anxiety. I was lucky that my job, which involved covering everything to do with the Brisbane Broncos, provided purpose and stability. I'd go down to training three times a week and the players would put me in playful headlocks to show me how much they liked me. To them, the headlocks were gentle. To the non-superhuman, it was a rigorous experience and required hours of physio a month. But they meant well and in their more candid moments they talked about how they dreamed of being 'abducted' into the Rugby League Hall of Fame. And if they didn't like one of your questions, they'd ask what you were 'incinerating'.

But by the time I got to Red Hill, the magic that had driven the Broncos to their second premiership the previous year had deserted them. They'd won only one game in the first month and struggled to win two games in a row for the first half of the year. Still, I was obsessed with their coach, Wayne Bennett. He had a column which I read every Saturday in *The Australian*. It wasn't about football. It was about life. Sometimes you'd get an even broader taste of his philosophies at training, where he'd tell players that if they wanted to point a finger, to do it at the mirror. 'The attitude has to be, "If we're not winning, it's my fault".'

And: 'The weak can never forgive. Forgiveness is the attitude of the strong.'

And finally: 'I don't do sad. I hate sad. Don't beat yourself up about things you have no control over.'

On the eve of the '93 Grand Final between the Broncos and St George, Bennett told his team he'd come into possession of the St George tactical tip sheet, which contained information written by Dragons coach Brian Smith on each of the Broncos players.

The tip sheet said that Glenn Lazarus was slow around the ruck, Trevor Gillmeister was overrated in defence, and Kevin Walters was the weakest of the Walters brothers, lived in halfback Allan Langer's shadow and was defensively fragile. Well, the Broncos played out of their skin during that Grand Final and won 14–6. A few years later, it emerged that Bennett had got hold of some St George stationery and written up the tip sheet himself.

After spending four months writing about the Broncos, I heard that Rupert had grown tired of *The Sunday Telegraph* (Brisbane Edition) and was going to shut it down. Even though no one in authority would confirm the rumour, I still felt like I was on death row when I went home every night – not knowing if I'd get a call the next morning telling me it was all over.

At the time I lived in a share house with Kylie, an old friend from uni, and her boyfriend, Shane. Kylie was making a fortune giving lap dances at Diamonds and Pearls in Petrie Terrace. All the girls at the club used pseudonyms, but Kylie just called herself 'Kylie'. She was good at her job and guys would follow her home and leave flowers on our doorstep. Shane tried his best not to get jealous. I spent hours convincing him that these offerings meant nothing to Kylie, when they actually meant quite a lot.

Our house was in Sexton Street, Petrie Terrace, opposite the old La Boite Theatre. Whenever the venue had a big play on, the opening night crowd would spill onto the street. One of these nights, the chat outside my window sounded familiar. I recognised the voices and laughter, so I peeked through the curtains and there, all glammed up and sipping champagne, were my classmates from drama school. They'd just performed their graduation showcase in front of Australia's top theatrical agents.

For 18 months I'd spent all day, every day with these people. We'd seen each other at our best and worst, and they'd made it through to the other side. And I hadn't. Not only that, forces had conspired to put me in this place at this time to show me the gulf between their lives and mine. How could they have all landed so conspicuously on their feet while my life was in limbo?

I couldn't even comfort myself in the knowledge that I had a cushy job decoding malapropisms because the jungle drums predicting the end of *The Sunday Telegraph* (Brisbane Edition) were growing louder. Then, one morning, the editor walked out onto the newsroom floor and said, 'That's all, folks.' Some journalists cried. Others were angry.

With only a few weeks of savings left, I planned to return to Cairns, lick my wounds and have another crack at finding a more permanent job. And that's when I ran into an old school friend in the Queen Street Mall. His name was Anthony and he'd graduated from putting on plays with me at Grammar to becoming a big-time ad director. He wanted to know how I was and I lied and said everything was great and I was really happy. He looked at me intently for a few beats, then said he was making an ad for a brand of mayonnaise and that I'd be perfect to play the role of 'Angry Man in Chicken Suit'. It was as though he'd seen right past my happy front and straight into my soul. Obviously I was concerned as to what kind of vibes my soul was giving out. But the deal made sense. I needed cash and he needed an angry man in a chicken suit. So I said yes and was cast on the spot. His only request was that I not call him 'Anthony' in front of the crew as his name was now Antoine. Antoine had apparently been able to do things Anthony could only dream of – which included dressing me in a chicken suit, sitting me on a dunking machine's collapsible seat, and dropping me into a pool of mayonnaise. It was embarrassing. Some of the crew called me a 'comedi-hen'. But it didn't matter because I had a plan. Within days of the ad money lobbing into my account, I'd packed my mustard-coloured 1974 Toyota Crown and was heading to Melbourne.

Kylie gave me the number of a stripper agency she said was always looking for drivers, 'in case you need cash'. I didn't know it at the time, but without that gesture, I wouldn't have lasted in Melbourne at all.

Australia A

By November 1994, Australia A's entry into the World Series Cup tournament was a reality. The originally programmed tri-series between Australia, England and Zimbabwe was now a 12-match quad-series. Up-and-comers like Greg Blewett, Matthew Hayden, Ricky Ponting, Justin Langer, Darren Lehmann and

Damien Martyn would suddenly get a chance to put their case to the selectors on the main stage instead of toiling away unnoticed in domestic cricket.

If you were Australian and under 25, there was no argument as to who you were going for. You might've loved Warne and the Waughs as if they were part of your family, but not when they were up against players closer to your own age. Cricket journalist Adam Collins wrote a story for *Wisden* about being ten years old during the tournament and barracking hard for Australia A. Decades later, he saw a man in a pub wearing a green Australia A shirt and offered him half his week's wage to buy it off his back. Collins wrote, 'He refused my offer. There was just no way he would part with that. They were his guys too.'

Jones was not part of the Australia A team when it was announced and it wasn't clear why he'd been left out. It couldn't be that he wasn't good enough. No one else that summer had been scoring triple centuries in the Shield.

Coach Greg Chappell said Jones was omitted because they were focusing 'an eye to the future'. Mark Taylor backed Chappell up, saying, 'Deano's unlucky to miss out. He's been punted against Ponting and Lehmann and missed out because he was 33 instead of 23. No matter how many centuries he makes this summer, that's one statistic he cannot change.' But if the youth policy was a requirement, then why was Merv Hughes selected when he was the same age as Jones?

'Surely what matters is not whether Jones is too old on paper, but whether his batting and fielding are still young and vibrant enough for the international arena,' wrote Greg Baum in *The Age*. 'No matter how it is dressed up by authorities, this team will be regarded as Australia's reserves, and look odd without Jones.'

When Jones was tracked down for comment, it was a 'no comment'. Baum concluded that Jones's exclusion from both Australia and Australia A was not because of age or form, but because he was just 'not wanted'. It must be hard when the country you nearly died trying to score runs for turns its back on you.

Australia and Australia A were both undefeated when they played their first match against each other at Adelaide Oval on 11 December. Australia A fans brought Australian flags with giant 'A's painted on them, and cheered relentlessly for 'the kids'. The best performers in that match were either already legends of the game or would become so. For Australia, Taylor (44) and Michael Slater (64) top scored, while Glenn McGrath (4–43) and Warne (3–40) got the wickets. And for Australia A, Hayden (45) and Ponting (42) top scored while Merv Hughes (3–33) starred with the ball. When Australia beat the upstarts by six runs, Mark Taylor was super annoyed that the crowd had barracked against the 'real' Australia. 'I didn't enjoy the game,' Taylor said. 'I don't like playing against my own players. I don't like it when the crowd doesn't support us when we play at home.'

I thought it was just a case of sour grapes from Tubby. I couldn't see his point at all. Now, I totally can. It was a lose–lose situation for the national side. If they won, it was expected. If they lost, then were they really the true national side? Still, the tournament kept getting more interesting. Michael Bevan was dropped from Australia to Australia A and scored a magnificent century against England to show the selectors what they were missing. The final game of the preliminary rounds between England and Australia A would decide who faced Australia in the finals. England needed to win, or score more than 237 to get over the net run rate required to finish higher on the ladder than Australia A. They did neither. They lost by 29 runs, scoring only 235.

The final series between Australia and Australia A was potentially embarrassing for the Australian Cricket Board. If Australia A won, then the selectors would be accused of not picking the best team to play for Australia and the whole industry built around the superstars of Australian cricket would be undermined. What happened next could be described as anti-competitive. The selectors took Australia A's best performing bowler, Paul Reiffel, out of the Australia A team and made him Australia's 12th man. It was a shitty act from administrators who'd created a concept that had got big on them. It got big on me too. I didn't know who I was in love with anymore. In the 17th over of Australia A's innings, when McGrath's elbow made contact with Hayden as the Queenslander was running between wickets, I was surprised how quickly I turned against McGrath. I mean, I was devoted to McGrath. I'd been on board since he had the *Dumb and Dumber* haircut and the hems of his trousers finished around his shins. Yet when he and Hayden 'collided' in the middle of the pitch, I was immediately on Hayden's side. For mine, McGrath had deliberately elbowed him – when he clearly hadn't. Both were ball watching. McGrath had his hands on his hips. Hayden simply brushed past his elbow as he was running by. But I was out of my seat. 'F U McGrath, you pig shooter!'

I wasn't alone. What had Australian cricket done to us?

At the end of that match, Ian Healy hit the winning runs off the final ball to guide Australia home and I was emotionally spent. I didn't invest in the second final, which Australia won by six wickets. It was time to get my head together and work out what was important to me. Which was Australia. And Australia A.

In 2016, 22 years after Jones's retirement and non-selection for Australia A, I was travelling around India, making a behind-the-scenes documentary on the T20 World Cup. Indian cricket fans always wanted to talk Australian cricket. If the chat was a quick one, you'd discuss Glenn Maxwell and Brett Lee; if it went for more than three minutes, you could be asked why Andrew McDonald didn't play more Tests. But in every conversation, a name hovered above all others, uttered with the reverence that Americans reserve for Kobe or MJ.

'Dean Jones.' 'Dean Jones.' 'Dean Jones.'

They knew his ability. So did the Australian selectors. That's why he didn't captain Australia A. If they'd won, too many people would've looked silly.

CHAPTER 5

The 1996 World Cup

'Shane, I think I'm pregnant.'

– crowd banner

After two days on the Newell Highway, I was in St Kilda. I'd never been to Melbourne before, but I'd heard St Kilda was cool and hoped some of it might rub off on me.

I parked my car outside the Oslo Hotel – 'Accommodation $100 a week'. It was a horribly cold, windy, rainy Melbourne day and Tex Perkins was walking down the other side of the street. He looked about as happy as I felt, but less terrified.

The hotel manager led me to my room. He had been the unfortunate recipient of an old-school hair transplant. About 15 hairs had been taken from the back of his head and plugged into the front, and at the base of each plug of hair the scalp seemed to rise up a bit, as if it was experiencing some sort of trauma. I wondered if something had happened to prematurely halt the operation or if he and his surgeon had agreed beforehand that 15 individual hairs would provide enough coverage.

My room at the Oslo was 2 metres by 2 metres. There was a massive sag in the mattress on the old spring bed, which had enough blankets to keep you from catching pneumonia but not enough to keep you from being cold. If you wanted a warm shower in the morning, you had to get up at 4 am, before the hot water ran out. Most days, as you walked down the corridor to the bathroom, you had to sidestep vomit.

The guy in the next room was Rob, 35. Just divorced. He'd sob loudly every night between 10 pm and 2 am. Some nights, the manager would knock on Rob's door and ask him if he was alright. Rob would say he was fine. And then the manager would say, as gently as possible, 'In that case, Rob, would you mind keeping it down?' Rob would say 'no worries'. Five minutes later, he'd be crying again.

I'd written to a bunch of newspapers and magazines before leaving Brisbane to try to set up interviews. Two had got back to me – *The Age* and the *Sunday Herald Sun*. The job I wanted was at *The Age*, the Melbourne broadsheet that once carried the writing of cricket journalist Peter McFarline – most famous for breaking the story of Kerry Packer's World Series Cricket takeover. My parents knew Peter and he'd come to dinner a few times in Cairns. During the 1982–83 Ashes, he'd gathered all the autographs from the Australian and England teams and sent them to me. I had those autographs framed and they sat on my bedroom wall for years. I studied them for hours and noted that the bowlers' signatures were flamboyant – Jeff Thomson's being the most flamboyant of all – whereas the signatures of the batters were generally contained and controlled, particularly the signature of GS Chappell. By the time I walked into *The Age* building in Spencer Street, Peter McFarline had been forced to work from his bed thanks to the debilitating spinal illness syringomyelia, but *The Age* he had described, the squat brown box of a building and the green carpet that led through the newsroom, was still there.

I was gripped with stomach-fizzing fear as I was taken into the editor's office. It was the day that Hurricane Marco had devasted South Jamaica, and the editor asked me what I thought of the Jamaica situation. I said it had struggled since the retirements of Holding and Dujon and was out of his office before his secretary arrived with a cup of tea.

I was less cowed when I arrived for my next interview with the editor of the *Sunday Herald Sun*, an amalgamation of the tabloid *The Sun* and the afternoon broadsheet *The Herald*, which my dad had worked for in the 1960s. If one staff member at the *Sunday Herald Sun* didn't like another, it was often because they came from 'the wrong side of the hyphen'. But the hyphen had been dropped off the masthead by the time I walked through its ramshackle newsroom with newspapers strewn everywhere and cacophony of loud, confident voices. 'Mate,' said a journalist into the phone as I passed, 'I'm not asking for a book. I just want a couple of quotes.' I kept walking down the corridor, passing Hawthorn star Shane Crawford, there to have his weekly column ghostwritten. Crawf smiled. I thought that was a good sign.

I sat down with the editor, Alan Howe. He was small. Early 30s. With a haircut that was almost a mullet, but not really. Kind of like Jeff Thomson around the time he told the media he liked hitting batsmen more than getting them out.

Alan was an Aussie who'd returned from working for *The Times* in London and was now one of Rupert's trusted lieutenants. He was also a big Beatles fan. Every week he'd write caustic CD reviews for the paper's entertainment section under the name 'Pete Best'. Here he is reviewing a Rod Stewart album: 'Let's hope this vapid tosh is the end. You're not in my heart. The first cut wasn't deep enough. I wish you were only joking. Do I think you're sexy? I think you're an idiot.'

I'd read the *Sunday Herald Sun* from cover to cover in preparation for the interview. But when I was sitting Alan's office, I had no idea he was actually 'Pete Best'. If I'd known, I'd have been more terrified. His steel trap of a mind and fast, staccato speech patterns were scary enough.

Alan: 'Date of birth?'

AZ: '13/1/72.'

Alan: '"American Pie" was number one that week.'

AZ: 'Right?!'

Alan: 'Favourite band?'

I looked on his wall and saw an impressionistic portrait of Paul McCartney.

AZ: 'The Beatles.'

Alan: 'Favourite album.'

AZ: '*Abbey Road.*'

Alan: 'You're hired. I'd have taken *Abbey Road* or *Rubber Soul*. Three days a week, starting tomorrow.'

At that moment the deputy editor, Lyall Corless, came in to start the interview, but it was too late – the die was cast. Lyall was a serious, hard-news man. And when he looked into my eyes, he knew exactly what I was – a soft-headed chancer who'd clog up the paper's system with overwritten human interest stories.

It was clear that if I was going to last, I had to learn how to write a story that was to Lyall's liking. So I studied his weekly pub reviews, which told me most of what I needed to know. Unlike Alan, Lyall wrote under his own name and his reviews were always no-nonsense information provided for your reading pleasure in the shortest possible sentences. Every week was the same: 'I had the steak. My wife had the chicken. The chicken arrived first. It was excellent. We washed it all down with Yalumba Family Reserve Shiraz ($20).'

One evening, Lyall and his wife dined at a well-known Fitzroy pub on gay night: 'Most of the clientele were young and generally pretty cool – something of a contrast to my forty-something jacket and tie and regulation short back and sides.' On this occasion, Lyall had the steak and his wife had the risotto 'which was excellent. Having finished our meals, we slipped away before drawing further attention to ourselves ... and headed straight to the Commodore.'

I learned some tabloid tricks along the way. For instance, subjects don't 'promise' things – they 'pledge' them. Someone doesn't 'criticise' someone else – they 'slam' or 'blast' them. A 'difficulty' becomes a 'hurdle'. 'Avoid' becomes 'snub'. 'Anger' becomes 'fury'. 'Controversy' becomes 'outrage'. An interviewee who strings together more than two sentences in a row can be accused of having an 'outburst'. If said interviewee strung together two sentences in a row in a previous interview, then it becomes the interviewee's 'latest outburst'. And no one 'says' things to a tabloid reporter – they 'admit' them, because it implies the subject crumbled under our cross-examination. It was fun to write and appealed to my sense of drama. But it also taught me habits that would take years to erase.

The forfeit

The 1996 World Cup, to be held in Sri Lanka, India and Pakistan, was meant to be 'The Redemption

World Cup' – the tournament that would make amends for Australia's disastrous 1992 campaign. But on 31 January, two weeks before the start of the tournament, 91 people died and 1400 were injured in a bomb attack in Colombo. The suicide bombing happened just metres from the hotel where the Australian team were booked to stay before playing their first match against Sri Lanka.

The Australians immediately decided that they didn't want to play in Sri Lanka. Steve Waugh suggested the match be moved to India or Pakistan. 'I'm not keen to go to Sri Lanka at this stage,' he said. 'I don't think anybody would.' The Department of Foreign Affairs and Trade wasn't keen on the team going either, recommending all Australians defer non-essential travel to the 'Resplendent Isle'.

But the Sri Lankan government was at pains to reassure the Australians that they would be secure. And when that wasn't good enough, it proposed flying them from India on a 'helicopter gunship' straight onto the ground at R. Premadasa Stadium where they would play the match before being flown back immediately afterwards. Ian Chappell, commentating on the tournament, thought it was a great idea. But Australian captain Mark Taylor wasn't receptive. 'We'd probably have to leave somewhere in India about four in the morning for the game. I don't see that as ideal preparation for our first game in the World Cup.'

Then came diplomatic representations through Canberra and a special briefing on security arrangements from the top brass of the Sri Lankan military.

The final option, to move the match to India, was rejected by the tournament organisers, who said that none of the four matches scheduled in Sri Lanka would be moved. 'The Sri Lankan government has told us they are in a position to hold the matches,' said Amrit Mathur, a spokesman from the organising committee. 'We have to stand by the decision since they are the co-hosts.'

Both sides held their ground, so ultimately Australia forfeited the match and Sri Lanka took the points without a ball being bowled. The path for Australia to make the quarterfinals was now more difficult. We'd have to win three of our four pool games against India, the West Indies, Kenya and Zimbabwe. There didn't seem to be any concerns among Taylor's men. They were confident they could do it. I wondered if they'd have been as happy to forfeit the match if they weren't the best one-day side in the world. Maybe if they thought they needed every point on offer they'd have been up at 4 am, boarding the helicopter gunship.

But our cockiness wasn't restricted to cricket.

When 22-year-old New South Wales all-rounder Shane Lee was selected in the squad, he was quickly taken under the wing of Shane Warne, with the promise that they'd 'pick up chicks' together. Warne had even thought up a name for the duo: 'The Shane

Show'. According to various interviews since the tournament, Steve Waugh did caution Lee about hanging out with Warne – a caution that fell on deaf ears. At the World Cup opening ceremony in Kolkata, every cricketer was accompanied by a model as they assembled on the ground. Warne saw it as the perfect opportunity for 'the Shane Show' to go to work.

'Warnie said, "I'll get the best two [models] for us – the Shane Show!"' Lee told the 'Betoota Advocate' podcast. 'Anyway, he lined up these two girls and we had one drink and we're going back to their place and we're thinking it's all going to happen. Then we got there and there's her whole extended family there and we spent the whole night signing autographs and having a bloody meal. I said, "Oh, the Shane Show, really Warnie?" And he goes, "Don't tell the boys!"'

Sheree

When my first pay cheque from the *Sunday Herald Sun* arrived, it was $400 – about $3000 short of being able to pay the bond on a flat and one month's rent. So I called the number Kylie had given me to see if I could get a job driving strippers. They said they had no jobs driving strippers, just driving escorts, and if I was interested I should turn up that night to an address in Melbourne's east and they'd see how I'd go.

At about 7.30 pm on a cold and windy Melbourne evening, I walked into a little office above a laundry.

On one side sat a bunch of middle-aged women (who would always be referred to as 'ladies') wearing corporate clothes and heavy make-up. On the other were a bunch of overweight men holding circa '96 mobile phones. The men were the drivers. They drank coffee and told each other bullshit stories while the women read magazines.

When the phone rang, the receptionist would put on a sexy voice and inaccurately describe the ladies she had on offer. Once their services were requested, the ladies and their drivers would head off into the night, determined and serious. I was paired with Sheree, blonde, slim, mid-40s. When the receptionist told her that I was to be her driver, she sighed. When we went downstairs and she saw the mustard-coloured Toyota Crown, she sighed again.

On the way to the job, apropos of nothing, Sheree told me that she thought I was going bald. 'Your hair's getting wispy and that's how it starts.'

Within a few minutes of knowing me, Sheree had diagnosed my greatest fear. I had an abundant amount of hair at the time, but my dad was profoundly bald. So all my life I'd been worried I'd go bald too. And the likelihood of that happening was being confirmed by a 44-year-old sex worker. Did Sheree have any experience in medicine? No. And it wasn't like she was trying to convince me that she was some sort of expert. She was just imparting information she knew to be fact. She may as well have been giving me road directions – which made the diagnosis all the more real.

Sheree: 'But don't worry. Bald guys make great sex buddies. Whereas hair guys are too cool and lack enthusiasm.'

AZ: 'I'd rather have hair than enthusiasm.'

Sheree: 'Really? Enthusiasm's pretty sexy.'

AZ: 'So is hair. You can't run your fingers through enthusiasm.'

A beat's silence.

Sheree: 'If you want to keep your hair, you should probably get on the meds before it's too late.'

The conversation soon moved from baldness to what my job entailed. She said I was to take her to the client's house, wait for the duration of the booking, then, if she didn't come out of the client's house within five minutes of the booking's scheduled end, it was up to me to go in and get her. I'd be paid $20 for a half-hour booking and $30 for a full hour.

I worked as Sheree's driver and security five nights a week. While she was with a client, I'd sit in the car, listening to the World Cup on the radio and praying she'd come out at the right time so I wouldn't have to mount a rescue mission.

I'd often pick up Sheree from her home, after she'd finished having dinner with her husband and put her kids to bed. At first, her husband wouldn't talk to me. He'd been let go from his job at the Ford plant in Broadmeadows and Sheree's wage was now supporting the family. His attitude improved when he realised I wasn't hitting on Sheree, and that I just wanted to raise enough money to get out of the Oslo Hotel.

One night, I drove Sheree from Melbourne to Ballarat so she could spend an hour with a service station attendant who'd saved all year to be able to see her on his birthday. I drove her and another client to Myer because it was the client's fantasy to be in a change room and have a woman change in front of him. I bought a copy of *Ulysses* because another client's fantasy was to have her stand in front of him in nothing but heels, reading James Joyce. Everything was on the table. Nothing was weird. Sheree explained that she preferred chubby clients because 'grinding on cushion feels good'. She hated big dicks because they'd put her out of action and affect her earnings. After a booking, she'd often walk extremely slowly from the client's house to the car and sometimes even hover outside the car for a moment before getting in. One night I asked her what she was doing. She said she was farting. She said the hardest part about escorting wasn't having sex with people she didn't find attractive, it was holding a fart in for two hours.

On the rare occasion that Sheree didn't emerge from her appointment at the designated time, I'd find a way to get her out unharmed. Unlike other drivers, my extractions involved gentle negotiation instead of threats of violence. Just the sight of a third party was often enough to shake a rogue client out of wanting to keep Sheree there against her will. But the spectre of violence was always around us. One night, not long after I started, Sheree didn't come out. So I knocked on the door of the client's house and a dude answered with a beer in his hand. He was about six foot, muscley, but also had a bit of a gut, and wore nothing but a towel around his waist. He looked at me as if to say, 'Yeah, I've got her, what are you going to do about it?' I could see Sheree behind him, concerned, and he had this look in his eye like he was going to do me some damage.

Then his face suddenly looked curious and he asked me if he knew me from somewhere. I said he looked familiar to me too. I didn't think he looked familiar, but I thought it might buy Sheree some time to come up with a plan to get out of there. He asked me if we'd gone to school or played footy together.

I said, 'No, but you definitely look familiar ...'

Then his face lit up. 'You're the fuckin' chicken! You're the guy in the fuckin' chicken suit that falls into the fuckin' mayo. My best mate and I laugh at you all the time.'

I confirmed I was. And while he was busy telling me the ad was 'so bad, it's good' and re-enacting the scream I made when I landed in the mayo, Sheree managed to sneak past him and run out the door. I bolted as well. The client ran after us, but he was momentarily slowed when his towel fell off, which gave us a chance to get in the car and drive away, leaving him on the street, naked. That was a fun night. We celebrated by getting thickshakes at McDonald's. At that moment, I thought I'd be working for Sheree forever.

The 1996 World Cup

Australia won the necessary three out of four pool games to book a spot in the quarterfinals, beating Kenya, India and Zimbabwe before going down to the West Indies. We had a solid top six in Taylor, Mark Waugh, Ponting, Steve Waugh, Stuart Law and Michael Bevan. Mark Waugh was in the form of his life and Ponting and Steve Waugh backed him up well. It was the bowling line-up which was forced to change after veteran spearhead Craig McDermott broke down with a calf tear against Kenya. It felt like the Queensland redhead had been around forever, but he was only 30 and one of the last links between Border's mid-80s strugglers and the super-confident line-up that felt it could forfeit games and still make the quarterfinals. Damien Fleming came in for McDermott and would turn out to be one of the top five performing bowlers in the tournament, as well as becoming Mark Taylor's go-to man to bowl at the death. As usual, Taylor's inventive captaincy and cool head more than made up for his slow scoring at the top of the order.

In the quarterfinal, New Zealand set an impressive target of 286, but Mark Waugh's 110 off 112 ensured the win, with 13 balls to spare. Mark Waugh's scores in the tournament were 130, 126, 76 NO, 30 and 110. So when we batted first against the West Indies in the semifinals and Mark Waugh was trapped LBW to Ambrose for 0, the bottom fell out of the Australian batting order. Taylor made 1, Ponting 0 and Steve Waugh 3. Suddenly, we were 4 for 15. Fleming said it was the first time in the tournament he'd heard the talk in the Australian dressing room become negative.

'It was a real tick to Curtly Ambrose,' Fleming later told 'The Greatest Season That Was' podcast. 'Just that moaning of, "He never gives us a bad ball. There are no half volleys." And I'm thinking, "Geez, this guy has got it all over us here."'

It was the younger members of the squad, Michael Bevan and Stuart Law, who pulled Australia's innings out of the dumpster with a stoic 138-run partnership that brought us to a mediocre, but defendable, 207.

Two and a half hours later, the West Indies were cruising to victory with left-hander Shiv Chanderpaul scoring 80 at the top of the order. They only needed 43 runs to win off 53 deliveries with eight wickets in hand. Then, weirdly, the Windies started hitting out. Once Chanderpaul departed, they collapsed, with Warne getting three wickets in three overs for just six runs. The champion leg spinner started the 49th over with a big leg break, which spun right across Ian Bishop's body and appeared to shave off stump. Warne went up, but the bails remained on. Warne's next ball was a well-disguised flipper, which wrapped Bishop on the pads. The umpire raised his finger and Warne stood for several beats after, his arms extended and his back arched – a man soaking in the glory.

Tony Greig: 'Well bowled, Shane Warne. He's come to the party when it mattered. That was a magnificent flipper.'

Curtly Ambrose was next in. The Windies needed 14 runs off ten balls with two wickets in hand. Ambrose and Richardson paddled Warne's next four balls for four singles, which meant Richardson was on strike for the final over, to be bowled by Damien Fleming.

Ten runs required off six balls.

First ball, Fleming was slightly short and Richardson slogged him over mid wicket for four.

TG: 'Richie Richardson is going to win this match for the West Indies. They needed that boundary. He's not going to leave it to the last ball, that's for sure.'

Six runs required off five.

Next ball, Richardson got an inside edge that trickled along the ground and Ambrose called him through for a single. Why? Why wouldn't you keep Richardson on strike? Healy deftly collected and threw down the stumps ... but it appeared Ambrose was safe.

TG: 'I think he got home. Ambrose has got long legs. Big strides.'

Then the replay of the incident was shown on the screen. Greig's co-commentator, Michael Holding, was suddenly concerned.

MH: 'This is close. Very close. As a matter of fact, it looks as if he's out.'

TG: 'He's gone, alright. Don't worry about that. That's all over.'

Meanwhile, on the field, Ambrose was so confident he'd made his ground that he wasn't even looking at the scoreboard's red and green lights, which were about to give him the news.

TG: 'He's not interested. He's not even looking at the lights, Ambrose. He's going to get the shock of his life.'

The crowd roared. Ambrose lurched around to face the scoreboard and saw the red light. I've witnessed slow exits from batters over the years, but this was the slowest. He ambled to the gate like a kid on his way to get the strap.

The West Indies were nine wickets down with six runs to get when the hatless, helmetless Courtney Walsh arrived at the crease.

TG: 'What's his form like, Michael?'

MH: 'Well, it's not the best, Tony.'

Richardson and Walsh spoke in the middle of the wicket. I'm no lip reader – and it was approaching 3 am Melbourne time – but I was certain Richardson's message to Walsh was 'get some bat on it and get off strike'.

Instead of doing the sensible thing and getting off strike, Walsh decided to try to book his team a final spot in one hit. He took a massive swing, missed, and Fleming's perfectly pitched delivery hit the top of middle stump. Australia was through to the World Cup final.

'We actually celebrated that night,' said Fleming. 'We went hard. We drank all night because we felt like we got out of jail.' Fleming would later say that it was those celebrations that inspired the booze ban for the 1999 World Cup.

It would be an Australia–Sri Lanka final. And Sri Lanka, who were unbeaten in the tournament, were out for revenge. Not only had there been the forfeiting debacle, which cost the Sri Lankans pride, but their 1995–96 tour of Australia had been one uncomfortable controversy after another. In the First Test in Perth, Sri Lankan players were accused, then cleared, of ball tampering. In the Second Test in Melbourne, Muttiah Muralitharan was no-balled by umpire Darrell Hair for 'throwing'. And finally, when Sri Lankan captain Arjuna Ranatunga claimed he had cramp and needed a runner in the second final of the World Series Cup, Australian wicketkeeper Ian Healy was rumoured to have said that 'you don't get a runner for being a fat cunt'.

Healy denies he said this. 'It didn't happen,' he told Channel Nine. 'What I said was, "You can't have a runner for being unfit." His reply was that he had cramp. And I said, "You've got cramp because you're fat. Have a look at yourself." And that was it. It wasn't nasty or anything. I don't like seeing the "fat cunt" line being written in books, it's horrible, and it's not true.'

Whatever Healy said, Ranatunga could be guaranteed to use it as inspiration to beat the Australians in the most-watched game in cricket history.

Neither Sri Lanka nor Australia had played in Lahore during the tournament. But one of the fundamental differences between the sides was that Australia didn't practise at night, so our players weren't aware of how much dew formed on the ground when the sun went down. It's times like this that Australia's confidence becomes its weakness: it was like we were too cocky for due diligence. If we'd trained one night in the lead-up to the game instead of always during the day, we would have known how difficult it was to grip the ball after dark.

Meanwhile, Sri Lanka *did* train at night and saw how wet the ground was. To get his team used to playing in the damp, Ranatunga ordered his spin bowlers to dip cricket balls in buckets of water before each delivery. Then, on the night before the final, Ranatunga left the official pre-function event early because he wanted to see if the dew on the ground had been a one-off. It wasn't. The field was soaking wet and it was then that

Ranatunga decided that if he won the toss, he'd bowl first. And that's what happened.

Ranatunga always said that if Sri Lanka kept the Australian total under 250, his team would win. Australia got off to a solid start with the bat. We were 1 for 137 when Taylor top-edged a sweep off Aravinda de Silva and was caught in the deep after making 74 off 83. That's when the momentum died. Between the 24th and 49th overs, Australia scored just one boundary. Shane Warne was even elevated up the order as a pinch-hitter but made just 2 off 5. We limped to 7–241 off 50 overs.

The Sri Lankans started their innings poorly, losing two early wickets. Then darkness fell and the dew started playing havoc with Warne and Mark Waugh. Both spinners towelled the ball down between deliveries but were still unable to get any grip and their combined 16 overs cost 93 without a wicket.

Asanka Gurusinha (65), de Silva (107) and Ranatunga (47) took the game away from the Australians. The dew must've also eaten at Warne's super-positive mindset because when Ranatunga struck a ball back at him on the full in the 43rd over, it busted through his hands and went for four. That was the wicket we needed to have any chance at winning. And it was one of five catches Australia dropped in Sri Lanka's innings.

Greig: 'I don't think Shane Warne will be feeling too good. You can see the look on his face – he's not enjoying this at all. So good against the West Indies and yet no real impression here.'

At the top of the 46th over, Ranatunga guided a McGrath delivery to the third man boundary and it was all over. Sri Lanka were World Cup Champions.

At the presentations, Mark Taylor didn't complain about how the wet conditions had hobbled his team. He told MC Ian Chappell, 'I think we were just outplayed. And they held their catches, which we didn't do.' Taylor then went to shake the hand of Pakistani Prime Minister Benazir Bhutto. She declined. Maybe it was a breach of protocol or etiquette. It was one of those nights for the Australian skipper.

The Sri Lankan team were booked to return to Colombo the next morning but managed to board a plane late that night with a bunch of delirious supporters. There weren't enough seats on the UL 320 Tristar, but it didn't matter. Players were desperate to celebrate at home, so they were allowed to sit on the plane's floor.

Goodbye Sheree

The *Sunday Herald Sun* was a magnet for celebrities. They'd either pop in to get their photo taken, be interviewed, have their column ghosted or complain to the editor about stories that had been written about them. A famous actor once walked out of the editor's office, saying, 'Merry Christmas and get fucked.'

Just two seats down from me sat a major celebrity ... well, Paul Stewart, the Painters and Dockers singer turned *Sunday Herald Sun* music writer was a celebrity to me. He was also funny. I was working late one night when I heard him on the phone to his eight-year-old daughter pretending to be 'Sergeant Perry from Fitzroy Police' and saying he'd witnessed her jaywalking that afternoon. The voice he put on was hilarious, and his daughter didn't buy it for a second. Of course, I was too shy to say g'day to the guy who brought us 'You're Going Home in the Back of a Divi Van', 'Die Yuppie Die' and the iconic 'Nude School'. In the end, it was he who approached me and asked if I'd be interested in interviewing musicians for a bit of extra cash, like $200 an article. He had a young family and didn't want to do interviews with international acts late at night. I tried to be cool, but my heart did skip a couple of beats. He'd just casually handed me my dream job, and $200 was what I got for a week of driving Sheree around.

My first interview was with Barry White, the velvet-voiced love god; the man who 'gets people in the mood' with hits like 'Love Serenade' and 'You're the First, the Last, My Everything'. And it happened while I was waiting for Sheree to complete an hour-long booking. I set up a little recording device that connected my phone to a tape recorder and was put through to Barry White via the *Herald Sun* switchboard. He'd just returned to fame thanks to his cameo appearances on the TV show *Ally McBeal* and wanted to tell me what a relief it was to be relevant again. 'The past 11½ years have been hell. Please believe me when I tell you that. For the past 11½ years, I have struggled in this industry. Until last year, I hadn't seen any results of my work. It was hard. It was very disappointing. I had to develop patience cos everything takes time.'

White didn't give answers to questions – he gave sermons. Each had two major lessons: success comes from hard work, and be good to your mother.

'I am concerned about people who are not doing anything with their life,' he said. 'I try to encourage them to get off their ass and do something. Don't just sit around waitin' all day for it to happen, cos it don't happen that way. That's what my mother taught me. She taught me everything I know. She taught me harmony. She taught me melody. At one stage, she wanted to teach me to read and write music. But I wanted to deal with music my own way. And she allowed me that freedom. The queen of my life is my mother, Sadie.'

When Barry hung up, I checked my tape recorder to make sure the words were all there – they were. I was now a music journalist, and I'd conducted my first interview while doubling as a sex worker's driver/security detail.

I looked at the clock. Sheree should've been out seven minutes ago. I hated this part of the job. I got out of the car and walked toward the client's house even though every cell in my body was telling me to stay away. I arrived at the client's door. Knocked. Silence. Knocked again. I heard footsteps. Then the client opened the door. He was early 40s, about 5'8" and wiry. No shirt. Hard face. A touch of the Bruce Lairds about him. He scrutinised me for a few beats, narrow eyes burrowing into mine. We both knew that he'd probably kill me in two and a half punches. A few seconds passed with us eyeballing each other ... then Sheree appeared.

She didn't seem to have been hurt or restrained in any way. In fact, she seemed relaxed and had a towel wrapped around her. She told me she'd get a taxi home. I asked her if she was sure. She frowned as if to say 'you're not my dad' then shut the door. As I walked back to the car, I heard them laughing.

Him: 'Is that your muscle?'

Her: 'He thinks he is.'

Him: 'Ha ha.'

Her: 'Ha ha.'

I resigned from the sex industry that night. I never said goodbye to Sheree.

When the next week's pay cheque rolled in from the *Sunday Herald Sun*, I finally had enough money to move out of the Oslo and into my own place.

CHAPTER 6

The 1999 Tour of the West Indies

'As captain, you can never be one of the boys.'

– Tony Lewis, *Playing Days*

In 1995, Australia won its first series against the West Indies in 20 years. It marked a reversal of fortune for the once untouchable Windies, and by 1999 they had slipped to sixth in the world rankings, were hampered by political infighting and had just lost to South Africa 5–nil. Likeable Jamaican fast bowler Courtney Walsh had been replaced as captain by the Trinidadian 'Prince', Brian Lara. At this time, Lara was considered the best batter in the world ... unless you were talking to Indians, in which case it was Sachin Tendulkar. But Lara's appointment had brought to the surface the traditional rivalry between the islands. The Trinidadians were exultant about it – whereas the Jamaicans didn't think Lara was a suitable replacement for someone of Walsh's standing.

'Being captain of West Indies is a huge honour and a huge job,' said former West Indies fast bowler and proud Jamaican Michael Holding. 'It needs a big man to do it, someone well-rounded as an individual. Brian Lara is not.'

For Australia, the captaincy transition from Border to Mark Taylor in 1994 was bloodless. And the transition from Mark Taylor to Steve Waugh in 1999 *seemed* bloodless. The message that filtered into the media was that the other candidates for the job, Shane Warne and Mark Waugh, were not considered because they'd supplied information about match conditions and possible team selection to a bookmaker in 1994. Waugh and Warne later admitted they had been 'naive and stupid' and were privately fined by the Australian Cricket Board in 1995. But the issue did not become public until 1998.

Mark Waugh seemed at peace with not being captain. Warne wasn't. He and his supporters believed he should have been appointed to the role and what had happened five years earlier with the bookmaker was irrelevant. From the outside, the idea that Warne would get the job seemed fanciful. Not because of the bookmaker incident. But because Steve Waugh was the Test vice-captain and one-day captain – so it would have been a surprise if Warne had leapfrogged him to get the job.

The more immediate problem was Warne's shoulder. He'd had major surgery the previous year – an operation doctors believed might kill his career – and now he was taking baby steps in his comeback. He'd played the final Test against England in January, picking up two wickets for the match compared to Stuart MacGill's 12. And the tour of the West Indies would hopefully let us know if there was a chance he'd return to his wizard-like best.

On a general level, the feeling going into the 1999 series in the West Indies was that Australia would win in a canter, the perfect soft landing for a new captain and champion in recovery.

Steve Waugh won the toss and batted in the First Test at Port of Spain. We were in a bit of trouble at 9 for 203, but the unlikely pair of Jason Gillespie, playing in just his 11th Test, and Glenn McGrath, who had an average of 4, put on a stand of 66 for the last wicket, bringing the Australian total to 269. The West Indies were then skittled by McGrath and MacGill for 167, losing their last seven wickets for 18 runs. Australia built on its 102-run lead thanks to Michael Slater's 106 on a difficult pitch for batting. Cricket writer Malcolm Knox described Slater's innings as a 'neglected masterpiece in the modern era'. Australia were bowled out for 261, leaving the West Indies 364 to win. The West Indies made 51 – their worst batting performance in their 71-year Test history. McGrath took another five wickets and Gillespie four. One–nil to Australia.

When the West Indies travelled to Jamaica for the Second Test, there were reports Lara had been partying at a Kingston nightclub called The Asylum until 4 am on the morning of Day 1 and missed the team bus to the ground.

At the coin toss, Lara told Steve Waugh, 'This is the last time I ever have to do this shit.'

Waugh walked into the dressing room and said, 'Oh they're gone. The captain doesn't even want to be here.'

Australia batted first, making a mediocre 256. The only resistance came from Steve Waugh's 100. We got a couple of early wickets in the West Indies' first innings before Lara made a quickfire 213 and completely took the match away from us. The only blotch on Lara's knock was when MacGill appeared to have him trapped in front on 99 and umpire Peter Willey gave him not out.

In journalist Adam Burnett's definitive oral history of that series for cricket.com.au, he described MacGill fielding at square leg when Lara was on 150 and umpire Willey saying to him, 'You thought that LBW was out when he was on 99, didn't you?' MacGill said he did. Willey grinned and said, 'Yeah, you're probably right.'

The West Indies were all out for 431. Australia responded with 177. The Windies won by ten wickets, equalising the series.

For the Third Test in Bridgetown, Steve Waugh thought one way to arrest the West Indies momentum was to ensure the Australian team was more focused, so he introduced a curfew. Burnett said Waugh blamed their performance in the Second Test on the fact that rum tasted better in the Caribbean, and believed the Australian side had become a little too in sync with the relaxed, carefree, partying vibe of the locals. The players grudgingly went along with the curfew.

Then Greg Blewett, who had top scored in two of Australia's four innings, was struck down with a thumb injury and Ricky Ponting was brought in to play his 23rd Test. When Waugh won his third toss in three matches and opted to bat, he and Ponting partnered for a massive 281-run stand, Ponting making 104, and Waugh 199 in Australia's 490.

The West Indies responded with 329 thanks to a century from Sherwin Campbell. That's when it all started to get interesting in the way cricket purists love but Australian fans loathe. Australia had a first innings lead of 161. But thanks to an epic 5 for 39 from Courtney Walsh, we were all out for 146, setting the West Indies a target of 308.

The West Indies second innings was in deep trouble at 5–105, and all seemed well in the world. Lara and Jimmy Adams then put on a 133-run partnership. But when McGrath took the wickets of Adams (38), Ridley Jacobs (5) and Nehemiah Perry (0), one after another, the Windies were suddenly 8–248 and 60 runs short of their target. Curtly Ambrose joined Lara, who stepped up the tempo. The pair added 54 before

Ambrose edged Gillespie to Matthew Elliott at third slip. This brought Walsh to the crease with six runs to win and no wickets in hand. But unlike the 1996 World Cup semifinal, the big fast bowler survived the onslaught from McGrath and Gillespie without losing his head before Lara collected the winning runs with a majestic 153 not out.

Australia's total of 490 was the eighth-highest first innings total in a Test match loss, which only made the defeat more gutting.

The West Indies led the series 2–1 and Steve Waugh was in danger of handing back the Frank Worrell Trophy, undoing all the hard work of captains Border and Taylor. Making matters worse, Gillespie had torn a disc in his back, opener Matthew Elliott's scores for the series were 44, 0, 0, 16, 9 and 0, and Shane Warne had figures of 2–134.

Depending on who you talk to, what happened next made perfect sense, or was the greatest act of treason in the history of Australian cricket.

Icons

Lyall knew I wasn't any good at the blood-and-guts stories that peppered the first 30 pages of the paper, so he'd get me to take stories that appeared in Britain's *Daily Mail* and adapt them to an Australian setting. This was called 'localising'. For instance, one week the *Daily Mail* carried a story about ten brave London firemen who would regularly rescue men who'd get their penises stuck in vacuum cleaners, washers and taps. So I tracked down Melbourne firemen who did the same job. The *Daily Mail* ran a story on 'London's Brightest Young Witches'. So I tracked down Melbourne's brightest young witches and wrote a double-page feature on them.

There was another story about politicians and how much they swear behind closed doors. To localise that, I rang Channel Nine's Canberra bureau and asked to speak to legendary political journalist Paul Lyneham. The voice on the other end asked why. I said I was doing a piece on politicians swearing. The voice said he'd been covering politics for nearly 30 years and why wasn't I calling *him* about politicians swearing.

I asked who I was speaking to and the voice answered, 'Laurie fucking Oakes'.

One day, Lyall asked me to localise a story in which the *Daily Mail* asked a group of ten prominent Britons to list their favourite icons from the twentieth century. When I made the same request to prominent Australians, most were gracious enough to help out. Gough Whitlam got the most mentions followed by Mickey Mouse, the lightbulb, the telephone, the television, Pablo Picasso, JFK and Diana, Princess of Wales. Surprisingly, Marilyn Monroe and Queen Elizabeth II didn't rate a mention. I asked Santo Cilauro, artist Mirka Mora, Phillip Adams, Maxine McKew, former leader of the Australian Democrats Don Chipp, Tex Perkins and former Victorian premier

Joan Kirner. Email wasn't in general use back then, so I had to cold-call, which I dreaded. Apart from Santo and Tex, they were all chosen to appeal to the boomer readership – and boomer editors – and there was one public intellectual that Victorian boomers loved more than any other, and that was former ALP president, cultural historian and *Pick a Box* champion Barry Jones. So I called him.

Adam Zwar: 'Mr Jones, we're doing a story on icons of the twentieth century, and I'm asking prominent Victorians to list five icons from the past 100 years that have meant something to them.'

Barry Jones: 'What are you talking about?'

AZ: 'Icons.'

BJ: 'Mm.'

AZ: 'Other people have mentioned Whitlam, Einstein, Muhammad Ali ... Mickey Mouse.' [Nervous laugh]

BJ: 'An icon is an image or statue.'

Curveball. But I kept my cool and thought fast.

AZ: 'Yeah ... but the language has changed to include people, hasn't it?'

BJ: 'An icon is an image or statue. The language hasn't changed – you're misusing the word.'

AZ: 'OK, let's forget about icons. Would it be possible for you to list five people or things you admire?'

BJ: (Yelling) 'NO. BECAUSE YOU'LL INCLUDE THEM IN YOUR RIDICULOUS LIST OF ICONS. AN ICON IS AN IMAGE OR STATUE.'

AZ: 'Mr Jones—'

BJ: 'I HAVEN'T GOT TIME FOR THIS. YOU'RE MISUSING THE WORD. GOODBYE.'

Click. Dial tone.

To this day, I don't know who Barry Jones's favourite icons are.

A few weeks after I'd interviewed Melbourne's brightest young witches, one of them wrote me a letter claiming I'd misquoted her and stating she'd put a spell on me. For the record, I didn't misquote her. I had a tape recording of her saying the exact words that appeared in the article. But now I had to put up with her random and completely unjustified spell, which just gave me another thing to worry about. I was folding up the letter and trying not to freak out when the phone rang.

AZ: 'Hello.'

Voice: 'Who's this?'

AZ: 'Adam Zwar.'

Voice: 'Sting.'

AZ: 'Sting? Wasn't I meant to speak to you in 45 minutes?'

Sting: 'You're speaking to me now.'

I started the interview unprepared and on the back foot. For about 90 seconds, Sting gave me a series of monosyllabic answers to questions about his new album. So I changed tack.

AZ: 'I understand your son is in a Police cover band?'

Sting: 'Bullshit. Absolute bullshit. My son has no interest in the Police. My son loathes the Police and so do I.'

AZ: 'OK. You're known for your great charity work—'

Sting: 'More bullshit. People think I'm the voice of universal concern. I only do two causes, Amnesty International and rainforests. That's all I'm involved in. No more, no less. Next question.'

I'm flustered. Cold sweat. I mention yoga, his passion. I knew if I could get him to expand on that for 45 seconds, I'd be able to regroup.

Sting: 'I'm fit. I'd run you around the block, I'll tell you that much.'

AZ: 'I'm sure you would.'

Sting: 'And probably beat you in a fight. What are you going to ask me about next? Tantric sex?'

AZ: 'Well ...'

A woman's voice came over the phone. 'Hi, your interview with Sting is over.'

I wondered if the witch's spell was already working. My next interview was with a vulnerable-looking Billy Idol at the Como Hotel in South Yarra. He was 46 at the time and feeling weird about it.

Idol: 'I've got good genes. I've been very lucky to have good genes. But I think it could be about to collapse at any moment, you know.'

He laughed that guttural Billy Idol laugh. I laughed with him. Self-deprecation. Maybe this interview was going to be fine. Maybe he liked me more than he liked *The Panel*'s Tom Gleisner, who he had tipped cold water over the night before.

Idol: 'Some people seem to think that I'm some sort of throwback act. I don't fuckin' think I am. The girls who go to our concerts are young.'

AZ: 'Really?'

My 'really' sounded too surprised and I instantly regretted it.

Idol shot me a death stare which belied the joyfulness of his fake tan. He then picked up my tape recorder and threw it out the hotel window onto Chapel Street.

I don't have the next bit recorded, obviously, but my notes said that Idol leaned back in his seat and continued talking as if nothing had happened.

Idol: 'Well, the girls that come to see me in America are young. I don't know what it's like here.'

If being a journalist had been my dream job, I'd have been happy to put up with rock star tantrums and witches' spells. But I wanted to be a filmmaker. And the reason I was working seven days a week – four days on general news and three days writing freelance features – was to save enough money to make a short film that'd be so successful it'd launch me out of journalism and into a TV career and everlasting happiness. But the money I was earning was never going to enable me to build enough of a nest egg to make a film. If that was to happen I needed to write for the *Sunday Magazine*, which appeared as an insert in the *Sunday Telegraph* and the *Sunday Herald Sun*, and paid eight times more than an article in the entertainment pages of the paper.

The editor of the magazine was an Englishwoman called Miranda who was tall and distracted-looking and didn't get on with many people. I think Miranda was probably shy and her shyness made her seem a bit up herself. She had a great eye for design and quickly dragged the magazine from colourful and bouncy to elegant and sophisticated. Her preference was to hire British writers to write celebrity profiles because she was convinced Australians couldn't write.

I kept pitching her articles and she kept saying no because nothing I was pitching had an 'angle'. I asked her what kind of an angle she was after. She said she'd know when she heard it. So that's when I pitched Miranda a story about Quan Yeomans, lead singer of the band Regurgitator. She said her readers weren't interested in Regurgitator, so I said my angle was that I'd grown up with him, had photos of us as kids, and our reunion would make a good story. The sceptical look on Miranda's face didn't change as she said she was 'half interested' but insisted that Quan had to acknowledge in the interview that he knew me. It couldn't just be me, as the narrator, saying, 'We hung out as kids'. I assured her he'd remember me. Only two years earlier, his mother had given me tickets to see Regurgitator support the Red Hot Chili Peppers.

I called Regurgitator's record company and arranged an interview. A few weeks later, I was sitting opposite Quan in the company's boardroom in Melbourne. He looked bored.

AZ: 'Hi. I grew up with you in Cairns.'

Quan: 'What's your name?'

AZ: 'Adam.'

Quan took a long, hard look.

Quan: 'No. No, I can't remember. I've wiped out a whole section of my life.'

Wow. So he didn't remember the days and weeks we hung out together, smashing snorkelling equipment in the garage downstairs while our parents had dinner. How was it that I had a crystal-clear recollection of his kung-fu obsession and his mum's beautiful cooking and his dad's white suits, and the fact that dogs gave him a rash, and he didn't even know I'd ever existed?

I ploughed on with the interview, asking the requisite questions until I could leave. I was certain I wasn't going to get paid for this and my career writing for the magazine was dead in the water. Then, as we wound down, Quan gave me a suspicious look.

Quan: 'You're not Adam Zwaaaaar? Did you used to have red hair and freckles?'

I told him I did.

Quan: 'I've got photos of you at home.'

Thank you, Quan. I don't want to overstate things, but that one bit of recognition would change my life.

The Fourth Test, St Johns, 1999

What was meant to be a glorified Caribbean holiday for the Australians had turned into a bare-knuckle fight. They were down 2–1 and had a Test to play. Shane Warne hadn't made an impact in the previous three Tests. Coach Geoff Marsh believed Warne still hadn't properly recovered from his operation.

Steve Waugh, who had loved being one of the lads throughout his 13 years of playing for Australia, needed to make a decision that might ruin a friendship but could potentially level a series and retain the Frank Worrell Trophy.

'You could certainly see Warnie wasn't at his best,' Greg Blewett told Adam Burnett. 'He was falling away to the off side in making that extra effort to get his shoulder over.'

Colin Miller told Burnett that Warne just didn't look threatening and West Indian opener Sherwin Campbell said the champion leg spinner could be relied on to bowl a few loose deliveries that could easily be 'put away'. That was harsh. And telling. No batter had ever spoken so dismissively about Warne before.

When Waugh and Geoff Marsh finally selected the team for the Fourth Test, they replaced Warne with Miller. Waugh said he wanted an off spinner to take the ball away from the Windies' five left-handers, which sounded sensible enough. What probably hurt Warne most was that fellow leg spinner Stuart MacGill's services were retained over his. MacGill was meant to be Robin to Warne's Batman, but MacGill had seven wickets so far in the series, to Warne's two.

In his book *No Spin*, Warne concedes he was 'bowling pretty ordinary' but still thought that Waugh should have backed him.

I remember seeing footage of the team doing a running drill on the morning of the Test and Warne, who'd already been told his fate, looked like all the life had been drained from his body. While the rest of the team skipped from witch's hat to witch's hat, Warne ambled and then walked, shoulders hunched, hat pulled down over his eyes like a kid who'd been told that instead of going to Disneyland, he'd be staying home to clean his room.

Blewett said Warne spent most of the game sulking. Miller said he could see Warne was 'very disappointed', a situation Miller needed to put out of his mind because he had a Test to play.

Warne immediately started talking about retiring. 'I'll have to think about things, about where I'm headed in the future,' he told *Sydney Morning Herald* cricket writer Malcolm Knox. Knox asked if he was considering retirement. 'Maybe. I'm not sure yet. It's something I have to think about. Financially, I'm pretty secure. I've got a beautiful wife, another kid on the way, a nice house, car, all those sorts of things. I've got a lot of business interests. Whether I want to get more involved in them is something I'll weigh up over the next few months.'

But Warne wasn't the only selection change for the final test – Blewett came in for the out-of-form Elliott, and Adam Dale replaced the injured Gillespie.

Steve Waugh won the toss, elected to bat and Australia made 303. Waugh top scored with 72 and Langer made 51, but the major talking point for the innings was Miller coming in at number 10 and making 43 off 38, hitting Ambrose for six into the jail adjacent to the ground. Ambrose still managed to snag five Australian wickets.

The West Indies' first innings was held together by Lara's third century for the series. He got to 100 in 84 balls, a feat made more remarkable because it took him 14 balls to get off the mark. His second 50 came in 21 balls, and he took 22 off a single Adam Dale over. Dale looked pale and exhausted and no one could work out why. Langer thought he needed to 'harden up'. But it would turn out that he actually had pneumonia and was hard enough to bowl through it.

After McGrath had Lara caught behind for an even 100, the West Indies lost 7–46 and were all out for 222. Australia had an 81-run lead going into the second innings.

Langer (127) and Mark Waugh (65) formed the backbone of Australia's second innings total of 306, leaving the West Indies 388 to win. They didn't actually need to win – a draw was enough to win back the Frank Worrell Trophy. But once McGrath trapped Lara in front for 7, the West Indies didn't offer much resistance and were all out for 211.

Frank Worrell Trophy retained. Curfew over. Australia's celebrations went into the night. Not for Adam Dale, though. All he wanted to do was go to bed.

After this test, Waugh went on to become Australia's most successful Test captain, and Warne the greatest leg spinner ever to play the game, taking 708 wickets and never, ever, forgiving Waugh for dropping him. You only need to tune in occasionally to the cricket coverage on Foxtel to know that Warne still feels like it all happened yesterday.

'It's tricky when you're good mates with a player you've got to drop, but you have to keep it professional,' says Mark Waugh, brother of Steve and close friend of Shane. 'We're all big boys. I mean, it didn't affect Warnie's career too much – he was a pretty good bowler after that. He might hold the odd grudge, Warnie, for Stephen, but I think it's just ... they're fine ... you just move on.'

CHAPTER 7

The 1999 World Cup

'I lost the World Cup. Nobody died.'
– Allan Donald

When the Australian cricket team arrived in England for the 1999 World Cup, the mood in the dressing room was still fragile after Warne's axing in the West Indies. So when coach Geoff Marsh announced to the group that there would be a total booze ban, it was received badly.

'Guys were just stunned, shaking their heads,' said Damien Fleming in 'The Greatest Season That Was' podcast. 'I often joke that Darren Lehmann started crying. He didn't, but he was bloody close.'

Steve Waugh also decided to start the tournament by using Glenn McGrath as a first change bowler instead of giving him the new ball. Waugh said it was an attempt to mimic what tournament favourites South Africa were doing with their spearhead, Allan Donald. But Donald didn't like bowling with the white

Duke ball and was able to control it better when the shine had worn off. McGrath had no such problem. In the end, all it did was unsettle the bowling group and put Australia on the back foot.

The first game was against Scotland. Steve Waugh won the toss and elected to bowl and the Scots were comfortable but slow against our highly rated attack. They made 7–181 off 50 overs and it took us nearly 45 overs and the loss of four wickets to beat them.

I didn't feel at all confident during the match. I was fidgety, chewing on pens and thinking about how embarrassing it'd be if we lost. In his book *Out of My Comfort Zone*, Steve Waugh remarked on the flatness of Australia's effort, saying he couldn't work out if the team was tired or tense. In our second game, against New Zealand in Cardiff, we won the toss and batted. Darren Lehmann (76) and Ricky Ponting (47) were solid, but none of our other batters really came to the party. After 50 overs we were 8–213. New Zealand, led by Roger Twose (80) and Chris Cairns (60), overtook our mediocre total in the 46th over. I clearly remember how relaxed and happy the Kiwis looked, whereas we seemed anxious and confused. In our third game, against Pakistan, we won the toss and bowled. Pakistan scored 8–275. I didn't know how Australia would get the runs because so far in the tournament, we hadn't threatened to score more than five an over. And when I saw Wasim Akram clean bowl Adam

Gilchrist, I didn't think anything would change. Akram (4–40) had control and variety. He swung the ball late, made it cut into the batter or simply yorked him. I didn't see how Pakistan could lose the tournament with him leading their attack. Mark Waugh (41), Ricky Ponting (47), Steve Waugh (49) and Michael Bevan (61) all offered resistance – just not enough of it. Australia's innings folded with one ball to go and 10 runs short of the Pakistani total. So with two losses and a win, we were suddenly in a position where we had to win every one of our next five games to make the semifinal. To dump even more pressure onto Steve Waugh, Chairman of Selectors Trevor Hohns told him that if Australia didn't make the semifinals, he'd be sacked as one-day captain.

So what does an Australian cricket team with its back against the wall do next? It makes the decision to give McGrath the new ball, immediately calls off the booze ban and brings back veteran all-rounder Tom Moody. Moody's selection in the World Cup squad had been to play the role of a sort of elder statesman and advisor to Steve Waugh. But in our next game against Bangladesh, he picked up three wickets and guided Australia home with a half century.

In our fifth game, against the West Indies, the old double act of McGrath (five wickets) and Warne (three wickets) re-emerged as they bowled out the West Indies for 110. And our batters coasted to victory in 40 overs.

Suddenly, Australia was into the next stage of the tournament. In lieu of quarterfinals, the organisers had come up with a complicated formula in which the top three teams from each of the two groups graduated into the next round called the 'Super Six'. There, they would play a round-robin format with the top four teams going through to the semifinals. But the catch was that points earned in the early part of the tournament were carried forward into the Super Six – and because Australia didn't have many of them, we had to win every game.

For Australia's Super Six clash against India, captain Mohammad Azharuddin won the toss and sent Australia in. Mark Waugh (83) and Gilchrist (31) started well, and the first seven Australian batters all got over 20 in a total of 6–282. McGrath was mighty with the new ball, dismissing the all-star trio of Sachin Tendulkar, Rahul Dravid and Mohammad Azharuddin. Australia won by 77 runs, the only blip being that Warne took a bit of stick. His 6.2 overs went for 49 runs.

We batted first against a resurgent Zimbabwe, but a stunning century from Mark Waugh (104) and 62 off 61 balls from Steve Waugh got Australia over 300 for the first time in the tournament. Zimbabwe's chase was courageous but fell 44 runs short. Warne (1–55 off nine overs) was ineffective again, and Steve Waugh heard rumblings that the champion leg spinner was still unhappy with being dropped in the West

Indies and losing out on the captaincy. So Waugh sought out Warne during a team stroll in Hyde Park, London. They talked through their issues and Warne also lamented that he wasn't able to be home for the birth of his son, Jackson.

Waugh instinctively knew the best way to extract a performance from Warne was to remind him that he was 'the man'. 'Shane needs ... support, encouragement and reassurance,' wrote Waugh. 'He loves to be loved.' When Waugh returned to the hotel, he seconded Tom Moody to look after Warne and keep his spirits up over the next few days.

South Africa was the number one ranked one-day side coming into the tournament, with a 75 per cent winning average between the 1996 World Cup and this one – 57 wins, 16 losses and three washouts. The team had become even more potent in recent months thanks to the devastating late order hitting of all-rounder Lance Klusener. Before 1998, Klusener wasn't an all-rounder; he was a fast bowler who could bat a bit. Then he injured his ankle and spent his recovery facing up to 600 balls from the bowling machine every day, working on his forward defence and refining his slogging. Klusener, a farmer who spoke fluent Zulu, said his practice method was about enhancing strengths rather than fixing weaknesses. It worked. During the 1999 World Cup, he'd come in to bat at around the 35-over mark and completely rip an attack apart. He struck the ball so hard the only way a fielder could stop it was if it had been hit directly to him. If the ball was hit a metre either side, he had no chance.

In Australia's final must-win Super Six game, South African captain Hansie Cronje won the toss and batted. Herschelle Gibbs scored 101 at the top of the order and Klusener did his thing at the back end, scoring a terrifying 36 off 21 balls to bring the South African total to 7–271. Shane Warne bowled superbly. It was as though the masterly control and zip that had made him the greatest wrist-spinner ever had returned after just one walk-and-talk with Steve Waugh. Warne picked up the wickets of Daryll Cullinan and Cronje. More importantly, his ten overs went for a miserly 33 in a high-scoring innings. But when it was the Australians' turn to bat, we suddenly found ourselves 3 for 48. Ponting's 69 off 110 balls steadied the ship and built the platform for Steve Waugh to play the boldest one-day innings in history. He defended, straight drove, slashed over point and slogged over mid wicket. He also sledged the bowlers. Maybe I hadn't been paying attention, but I'd never really seen an international batter so pointedly intimidate the opposition attack. Waugh said to Cronje, 'I'm taking you down today.' The South Africans already called him the Ice Man and he was more than living up to it. Waugh would later write that he was in complete battle mode 'to the point of being arrogant'.

There had been a small event leading up to the game that became significant. Shane Warne had put his hand up toward the end of Australia's pre-match team meeting and told the group that 'if anyone hits the ball in the air to Herschelle Gibbs and he catches you, don't walk straightaway, because he has a habit of showboating and he might drop it in the process'.

So when Waugh, on 56, mistimed a flick off his pads and gently lobbed the ball to mid wicket, the vision shows Gibbs move slightly to his right and catch hold of the ball ... but only for a fraction of a second, before trying to toss it up in celebration and losing control of it in the process. The event unfolded just as Warne had predicted it would, and Waugh stood his ground. Not out. Commentators Tony Greig and David Gower analysed the slow-motion footage.

Tony Greig: 'He's about to throw it up. And that's it. You could almost make a case for the fact that he probably caught that.'

David Gower: 'Afraid not.'

Waugh then said to Gibbs, 'Hey Herschelle, do you realise you've just cost your team the match?' But that day, after the professionals in the press box punched it up, the sledge became 'Hey Herschelle, you just dropped the World Cup.' The throwaway comment has been repeated and reappropriated on cricket grounds and in bars all over the world for 22 years and is almost as famous as Steve Waugh himself. A shame he didn't actually say it.

Australia went on to win with two balls to spare and book a place in the semifinals. The match would be in Birmingham in four days' time. And this time our opponent would be ... South Africa.

My final general news shift

It was tough to get anything in the paper on a Saturday night. Alan Howe, proud of all the work that had been done during the week, would say there needed to be a double murder to edge out stories that had already been placed in the first edition. And when the Collingwood fanatic editor said 'double murder', it was interpreted as two people getting killed, or any infraction involving a player or official from the Carlton Football Club.

So when a 'source' rang to say that Carlton President John Elliott had been busted drink-driving, there was unbridled elation in the Collingwood-centric newsroom. Lyall, also a Collingwood supporter, immediately sent me down to the Elliott mansion in Toorak to obtain a quote.

At 10.40 pm, with the presses due to roll on the second edition at 11.30 pm, I was standing outside Elliott's front gate, staring at the intercom. What was I doing? I wasn't a hard news reporter. Foot-in-the-door journalism wasn't my thing. I struggled to introduce myself to people even in the most hospitable of environments, so what was I doing trying to instigate a conversation with a stranger in the middle of the night? Also, I didn't care that John Elliott was busted drink-driving. I would've turned the page if I saw the story in any paper I was reading. And that's only partially because I'm a life-long Carlton supporter.

I stood staring at the button for about 30 seconds. Then I called Lyall and said I'd tried the intercom and no one had answered. 'Try again,' he said. So I tried to shut down my mind like I'd taught myself to do when attempting to protect Sheree from rogue punters. I approached the intercom, closed my eyes and pressed the button. A woman answered – it was John Elliott's then wife, Amanda.

AZ: 'I'm so sorry. My name's Adam Zwar. I'm from the *Sunday Herald Sun*. We've heard that your husband may have been caught drink-driving. I was wondering if he was there?'

The intercom buzzed. This was unexpected. I hesitated. There was an arm wrestle going on in my brain between the fear of walking through the gate and the fear of Lyall's wrath. Lyall won. I walked through the gate and approached the door. Before I could knock, Amanda Elliott had opened it, a worried frown on her face.

Amanda: 'He should have been home hours ago.'

AZ: 'Right.'

Amanda: 'Oh my God, I'm actually quite concerned. Have the police got him or what?'

AZ: 'I don't know.'

Amanda: 'It would just be nice to know where he was. What do the police do when they pull you up for drink-driving?'

AZ: 'I don't know. I don't even know if he has been pulled up drink-driving. It's just a rumour.'

Amanda: 'It's probably right. He's in as much trouble with me as he is with the police. I can't imagine where he's gone. Unless, God, I don't know ... surely not the casino again. If you run into him, tell him to come home. Maybe he can't get home ... he can always ring.'

This was devastating. I was silently willing her not to open up so much. After a seven-minute chat, I went back to the car, called the *Sunday Herald Sun*'s copytakers and filed my verbatim conversation with Amanda Elliott.

There were cheers when I got back to the office. Here I was, a dyed-in-the-wool Carlton supporter with zero interest in bringing down my club president, being treated like some kind of hero. Staffers who'd ignored me for three years approached and introduced themselves. 'Great stuff.' 'You nailed him.' 'Where you from, mate?' Lyall even lauded my efforts and shouted me a beer at the pub. Or did I just imagine that?

Next morning, as I went to buy the paper, I saw a woman in her car stopped at traffic lights near Como Park. She looked familiar. Thick hair. Toorak-y. Almost too well presented for a Sunday morning ...

Then I noticed she was crying. And then I noticed the woman was Amanda Elliott.

I had no appetite for this kind of reporting. I just wanted to write about fluffy showbiz stuff with a view to one day being professionally involved in fluffy showbiz stuff. But if I was going to do that, and exempt myself from the stresses of foot-in-the-door journalism, then I would have to go freelance. Words abandoned me when I sat down to explain my plan to the chief of staff. I feared if I left general news, the hierarchy would think I was turning my back on them and no longer accept my freelance contributions. Disloyalty at that organisation always resulted in being blacklisted. But the chief of staff quickly got a handle on what I was trying to say and cut to the chase.

COS: 'Look, Adam, we're happy with what you're doing here ... for the most part. And you could be a good general news reporter. But you've got to decide what you want to be, an actor or a journalist.'

My mouth started speaking before my brain kicked into gear.

AZ: 'I want to be an actor.'

COS: 'Well, lose some fuckin' weight and go and do it!'

Alan, Lyall and the chief of staff couldn't have been more delighted I was going, as it meant they could bring in a proper hard news reporter to replace me. It was during this state of mutual celebration that we struck a deal where I'd be able to keep my security pass and have a desk in the newsroom as long as I wrote exclusively for News Limited. So I packed up my desk and went home happier than a leg spinner with two pizzas.

The World Cup finals

After the heroic come-from-behind win against South Africa in the final match of the Super Sixes, Australia were now facing off against South Africa in the semifinal. But this time we lacked intensity. It was as though we'd reached our peak four days earlier and were now spent.

Hansie Cronje won the toss and sent Australia in. We soon found ourselves 4 for 68 after South Africa's fast bowlers Allan Donald, Jacques Kallis and Shaun Pollock ripped through the top order. This brought Steve Waugh and Michael Bevan together again to steady the ship. They needed to keep the runs ticking over, but not take risks because all that was left after them was Tom Moody and the bowlers. Steve Waugh was exhausted from the previous game, so he gave himself a pep talk – he knew if he and Bevan could hang around they might be able to get Australia to a competitive 220. In the end, they both made half centuries and we were all out for 213.

In those days, 213 might've been defendable in some situations, but not in a World Cup semifinal against a batting line-up that included Gary Kirsten,

Herschelle Gibbs, Jacques Kallis, Darryl Cullinan, Hansie Cronje, Shaun Pollock and Lance Klusener.

By the 12th over, South Africa were coasting, with openers Gibbs and Kirsten taking their total to 48. Waugh needed a circuit-breaker, so he threw the ball to the resurgent Warne, who pounced on Gibbs, bowling him with his second ball. It pitched almost seven centimetres outside leg stump and went on to clip the top of off. It was magic. Adam Gilchrist said the delivery was equal to Warne's 'Ball of the Century'. Perhaps the Gatting ball spun a fraction sharper. As Gibbs turned to walk off, Warne charged his teammates as they went to embrace him and it took a wall of them to stifle his forward thrust. 'His drive and will were literally scary,' Waugh wrote. 'But he scared life into others who were tensing up under the South African onslaught and got us back into the game.' Warne would take the wickets of openers Kirsten and Gibbs, as well as captain Cronje and champion all-rounder Kallis. It was as though the months of humiliation and rejection had helped Warne get an otherworldly amount of revolutions on the ball, bamboozling four of South Africa's best batters. There was no doubt he was 'the man'. But when he finished his ten overs (4–29), the match swung again toward South Africa, with the fast-scoring Shaun Pollock looking like he was going to get the Proteas home. But when Fleming bowled Pollock and McGrath bowled Mark Boucher, we were suddenly back on track. Or were we? Once Klusener arrived at the crease, he immediately piled on the boundaries. In the commentary box, Bill Lawry was riding every delivery. 'That's hit like a rocket. That's four.' And then, 'What kind of shot is that?'

When Klusener whacked Fleming through mid wicket bringing up 180 for South Africa, Lawry couldn't disguise his feelings.

Bill Lawry: 'Oh he's gone for it. And it's gone. It's gone. Oh dear! Four. Beautifully struck.'

Former South African all-rounder turned commentator Mike Procter responded: 'I don't know about "oh dear", that's a fantastic shot, Bill.'

In the second-last over, when Reiffel ran out Steve Elworthy, it brought a slightly stunned looking Allan Donald to the centre. The crowd noise was deafening. Sixteen runs were needed off the last eight balls with no wickets in the shed. Klusener slogged McGrath's next delivery in the air to deep mid-on, the ball going so fast that it pierced Reiffel's normally safe outstretched hands and went for six.

FAAAARK!

Then Klusener got a single off the last ball to retain the strike. I was on the phone to a mate, who was also watching. We were silent.

Fleming came on to bowl the final over. South Africa needed nine to win off six balls. A tie meant Australia would go through to the final, thanks to our stronger net run rate.

Fleming bowled the first two deliveries around the wicket, yorkers outside off stump per the team's predetermined plan to bowl to Klusener. Klusener sent both balls to the boundary. Scores level. Four balls to go. Barring a disaster, South Africa had this in the bag. Fleming told Waugh he was going over the wicket and Waugh backed him.

On the broadcast, there was a tight shot of Warne looking like the grumpiest man alive. Next ball, Klusener clubbed it to Darren Lehmann at mid-off. Donald had backed up too far and was way out of his crease when Lehmann shied at the stumps and missed. If he'd hit, Donald would've been out. Game over. Australia through to the final.

Bill Lawry: 'Donald was backing up and that would have been a tie. Can you believe it? I cannot believe it.'

This was hard to watch. A resolute Fleming went back to his mark. Fourth ball. Yorker. Klusener hit it to mid-off. This time, a gun-shy Donald didn't back up. Klusener was already halfway down the wicket when Mark Waugh flicked the ball to Fleming at the bowler's end ... but Donald was still in his crease, so Fleming immediately rolled the ball along the pitch to Gilchrist at the striker's end as Donald suddenly made a run for it. He was only halfway down the wicket – without his bat, which he'd dropped – when Gilchrist broke the stumps. *TIE.*

Bill Lawry: 'That it. South Africa are out. Donald didn't run. Oh I cannot believe it. Australia go into the World Cup final. Ridiculous running with two balls to go.'

My friend and I were screaming into the phone. I'd followed the Australian cricket team for 19 years and this was my greatest ever moment.

Conversely, in the Australian dressing room afterwards, the celebrations were muted. 'There was silence, there was disbelief, which after 30 or 60 minutes turned into something a little more jovial,' Moody told 'The Greatest Season That Was' podcast. 'But still it was nothing like what people might expect. Because I think we were still in shock.

'There was a few of us who met in the hotel bar for a token drink. But the job wasn't done.' An in-form Pakistan was waiting for them in the final.

As a fan, I didn't know how much energy I had left in me. Wasim Akram won the toss and elected to bat. The Australian side had gone through a full transformation since it had played Pakistan earlier in the tournament. It was now highly drilled, and aggressive. McGrath struck early, finding the edge of opener Wajahatullah Wasti, and Mark Waugh flew horizontally to take the catch. Then Fleming, Reiffel and Moody all chipped in, but it was Warne, back to his pre-shoulder-surgery best, who blew the Pakistan innings apart, taking 4 for 33. Pakistan were all out in the 39th over for 132. Mark Waugh, Gilchrist, Ponting and Lehmann combined to chase down the runs in 20 overs.

Worst World Cup final ever? Probably. I was happy, though. To me, the final was like the Champs-Élysées stage in the Tour de France. Australia had rebounded from being listless also-rans on the edge of being booted out of the tournament and their captain sacked, to undefeated in their last eight games. Now it was time to pose for photographs in their yellow jerseys and enjoy a glass of champagne.

CHAPTER 8

The 2001 Tour of India

'What is human life but a game of cricket?'

– John Sackville, 3rd Duke of Dorset, 1777

On the night of the 2001 Allan Border Medal, Australian cricket had every reason to celebrate. The men's side had won a record 15 Tests in a row, obliterating the West Indies' previous record of 11. We were the reigning World Cup champions and our domestic competition was the envy of the world. What's more, fortune had given us a team with at least five players who would be legends in any other team in any other era – the Waughs, McGrath, Warne and Gilchrist. And Matthew Hayden was about to come into his own.

If there was one job left for Australia in world cricket – one territory to conquer – it was India. The last time an Australian side won a series there was Bill Lawry's 1969 team. Since then, India had been a miserable experience for successive Australian touring parties, who rarely left the hotel and just wanted to get in and out without a severe gastro incident. Steve Waugh bucked the trend. His philosophy was that the only way to win in India was to embrace its culture and people. On the 1998 tour, it was team policy to not leave the hotel, but Waugh didn't let that hold him back. He snuck out of the hotel on 25 separate occasions and arranged for tour guides to take him on excursions, day and night. It was a trip to a rehabilitation clinic for leprosy-affected children that led Waugh to take his first steps in what would become a life of charity.

The Allan Border Medal was the Australian men's team's last chance to let off steam before getting on a plane to Mumbai for the 2001 Border–Gavaskar Trophy. Colin Miller won Test Player of the Year, Glenn McGrath won One Day Player of the Year, and Steve Waugh the Allan Border Medal. As the credits on the broadcast rolled, Jimmy Barnes and his son David Campbell came on stage and belted out the Cold Chisel classic and unofficial anthem of the Australian men's cricket team, 'Khe Sanh'. Then, from the dining area, cameras caught the lone figure of Michael Slater gliding through the audience toward the stage with a glass of red in hand. The broadcast cut to Adam Gilchrist, who laughed and applauded as Slater walked on stage. Slater wrapped an arm around Barnes while Campbell looked at his father as if to say 'Are we really doing this?' But Barnes made Slater feel welcome by sharing his microphone with him as the 'Khe Sanh' duo became a trio. If the viewers at home had a representative that night, it was Andrew Symonds. When the broadcast cut to him, he was grinning ... but there was also a look in his eye that suggested this wouldn't end well.

Slater later said in his autobiography that getting drunk at the Allan Border Medal and walking on stage was a reaction to an incident that had happened the day before, when Australian Cricket Board chief executive Malcolm Speed pulled him aside and said he'd heard the opener had a serious drug problem.

'Cocaine, heroin ... that sort of thing,' Slater quoted Speed as saying.

Slater told Speed, 'You go back to your so-called reliable source and tell him he's not so reliable. Drugs have never been a part of my life, will never be a part of my life. It's just something I will never stand for.'

Slater said he suspected he'd been thrown under the bus by a teammate, but he couldn't prove it. His response instead was to get drunk and storm the stage.

A week or so later, the Australian team flew to India and although the rumblings about Slater were growing louder, they were drowned out by something much bigger.

Miranda

After the article on Quan, I'd become a regular contributor to the *Sunday Magazine*, interviewing every international superstar who came to Australia to flog a stiff movie, album or book. In those days, that was the only reason a superstar would come to Australia. Miranda even asked me to write a column about being a single man. It would mean an extra $2000 a week and give me a proper creative outlet and a nationwide profile. She made it clear my voice was 'exactly' what the magazine was after, and asked if I'd mind writing a 'dummy' column to give the art department an idea of my tone. So I wrote it, sent it in – and there was silence. When I say 'silence', not only did I not hear from her about the column, I didn't hear about writing any more features either.

Weeks went by and I started running low on money, and there weren't many other avenues to make up the shortfall. The *Sunday Herald Sun* entertainment section had cut back on contributors and there was no acting work to speak of. I'd had a short burst of acting jobs when I first went freelance, making guest appearances as crooks on *Neighbours*, *Blue Heelers* and *Stingers*, which were all shot in Melbourne. Now I had to wait the regulation two years for the audiences of those shows to forget about me so I could come back to play another crook. The only gig that came my way during this period was modelling for an anti-drink-driving pictorial campaign, where I played the hospitalised victim of a drunk-driver. I spent a morning in the Alfred Hospital's intensive care unit being photographed wearing a neck brace and what make-up artists call 'Car Crash Face', while people with *actual* broken necks and faces affected by *actual* car crashes lay disapprovingly nearby. The resulting image went on billboards, the sides of trams and the backs of taxis all over Victoria. Although the job paid nearly a month's rent, seeing me like that really upset Mum. And it's not like things were going well for her.

Mum's breast cancer had been in remission, but she was now experiencing pain in her ribs. Her oncologist diagnosed her as having osteoporosis, but the medication wasn't giving her relief. He'd X-rayed her but didn't think an MRI was necessary, even though it's common for metastatic breast cancer to appear in the bones. Mum and Dad, who were now living in Beechworth in north-eastern Victoria, would make long road trips to see the specialist. Three hours there and three hours back just so he could insist that her acute pain was nothing to worry about.

So I was possibly feeling a little down when I got into the *Herald and Weekly Times* lift one Friday afternoon and an officious security guard put out his hand to stop the doors from closing and spoke to someone standing outside the lift. 'Madam, this lift is going up. You should take it.'

I couldn't see the woman he was talking to, but she was clearly indicating she didn't want to take the lift. Why wouldn't he let us do our own thing?

'Please, madam, it's going up.' The expression on his face changed from concern to relief as a grumpy-looking woman entered the lift. It was Miranda. It had been three months since we'd last spoken. We rode up in silence for the first couple of floors. She wasn't going to talk, so it was up to me. I told her I didn't care that she didn't like my column.

'It's not like I didn't like it,' she said. 'I just thought you were trying too hard.'

I agreed.

'You've also got to watch your tautologies,' she said, not letting up. 'All "agreements" are "mutual" and all "disasters" are "major". And I'm sorry your friend "died" of a "fatal" drug overdose. But if he died, the reader assumes the drug overdose was—'

'I get it.'

The lift doors opened and she exited. The burn was made worse by the confident way she hit every consonant. I stared up at the mirror on the ceiling of the lift. It was clear I'd lost more hair since I'd last looked.

If I'm guessing, I think Miranda might've felt that she'd come on a bit strong because when I got back to my desk, she'd already sent an email offering me two assignments for the following Wednesday. She said a car would collect me from my house in the morning and take me to a record company office in west Melbourne to interview Jimmy Barnes fresh from his moment with Slater, then on to the airport where I'd be flown business class to Stuttgart to interview AC/DC. 'Please confirm.' I read the email again. Car.

Barnes. Business class. Stuttgart. AC/DC. I'd earn more in a week than I'd earned in the past three months – all thanks to a security guard with an aversion to partially occupied lifts.

Slater, Bradman and the First Test

It was a Sunday morning in Melbourne and I was writing an article at my computer with the television on silent when I looked up and saw regular programming had been interrupted by that iconic black-and-white footage of Don Bradman hitting a golf ball against the corrugated exterior of a water tank. I knew what that meant. The chyron confirmed it: 'Donald Bradman dead at 92.'

It was 3 am Mumbai time when members of Waugh's team were woken in their hotel rooms by calls from journalists in Australia asking for comment on Bradman's passing. When the team went downstairs to breakfast at 6 am, Steve Waugh said 'every second person' at the hotel approached him and his teammates to say how sorry they were. Adam Gilchrist was particularly moved by their commiserations.

'The staff in the hotel were all just so apologetic,' Adam Gilchrist told 'The Greatest Season That Was' podcast. 'They were coming up and saying their condolences. There was this grieving going on. They were treating us like he was our father or grandfather.'

Waugh said it was like 'India was in mourning' and there was talk from Indian officials about postponing the First Test so the Australian team could deal with the loss. Waugh politely declined, saying, 'Sir Donald wouldn't have wanted that.'

The reactions of the Indians revealed a cultural difference, in that there's a practice of national mourning in India, whereas Australians reserve their mourning for friends and family. With few in the team ever having formed a personal friendship with Bradman, his death served only to put more pressure on them. Steve Waugh said it cast 'a mighty shadow' – and part of that was constantly being asked to talk about someone who was better at the game than they were.

Bradman averaged 99.94 in Test cricket, scoring 29 centuries in 80 innings, but his career mainly existed in statistics or on grainy black-and-white footage shot at 24 frames per second. If there was a moment that made the Don relatable to the modern fan, it came during the rest day of the Fifth Test in Adelaide in 1978. A 69-year-old Bradman attended a dinner at the house of Dr Don Beard – a well-known Adelaide surgeon and doctor to generations of cricketers. Also attending the dinner were Jeff and Cheryl Thomson, former Australian off spinner Ashley Mallett, Indian opener Sunil Gavaskar and the left-arm orthodox bowler Bishan Bedi. One of the features of Dr Beard's backyard was a professionally curated turf wicket. That afternoon Dr Beard's sons, Matthew and Alastair, were having a hit and asked

Bradman if he would like to join them. Bradman, who hadn't held a bat in 20 years, said he'd love to. And that's when Jeff Thomson put down his drink and said, 'If Bradman's batting, Thomson's bowling.' Mallett said Bradman batted against Thomson for 20 minutes and belted 'the hell out of him'.

'Didn't miss a ball,' Mallett told *The Advertiser*. 'No box, no gloves, just the boys' bat and quite lively bowling. Thommo reckons he was bowling leg breaks but his leg breaks are about Dennis Lillee's pace, so they're quick. He was the quickest bowler who ever lived.'

Thomson would later tell Mallett in his book *The Diggers' Doctor* that he just rolled his arm over at first. 'But then I realised that Bradman's strokes and dancing feet were still there, so I quickened my pace, but to no avail ... That little old guy in glasses was suddenly transformed into Don Bradman, the human thrashing machine. He did not play a false shot in 20 minutes of the most amazing batting I've seen.'

At the end, Bradman and Thommo walked to dinner arm in arm with Bradman telling the fast bowler: 'You know, Jeff, I enjoyed that knock, but I'll never do it again.'

So Bradman could bat. He was a hard-headed administrator. And he was funny. On Day 2 of the Fifth Test against the West Indies in Adelaide in 1989, an 81-year-old Bradman saw a sublime 216 from Dean Jones, backed up by a big-swinging 72 from

Merv Hughes. In the dressing room after play, Hughes was being showered with cans of XXXX following his improbable innings. But when Bradman went down to the rooms, he only had eyes for Jones, and the two had a respectful chat – batter to batter – before shaking hands and nodding at each other earnestly. Then Bradman turned and saw Hughes, who seemed to be eagerly awaiting his congratulations from the great man.

'Merv Hughes,' said Bradman as the big fast bowler's eyes lit up. 'Seventy-two not out in a Test match.' Then he added: 'Funny game, cricket.'

So it was under the spectre of Bradman's passing and the question mark over Michael Slater's eccentric behaviour that Steve Waugh won the toss and bowled in the First Test in Mumbai. The gamble paid off with Warne (four wickets) and McGrath (three wickets) bundling India out for 176, and it wasn't long into the Australian innings that Matthew Hayden started to stack on the runs.

My fingers were crossed for Hayden. I wanted him to cement a spot in the team. He'd racked up billions of runs in Shield, but struggled in Tests. This tour felt like his last chance, and India was the last place you wanted to be taking a last chance. The pitches are slow with inconsistent bounce, particularly after Day 2, when the extreme heat eats away at the surface and large cracks appear in the turf. Slow bowlers use these cracks to get the ball to grip and turn which can make even the most prodigious of batting talents look foolish.

Hayden had prepared. Before the tour, he organised with the curator at Allan Border Field in Brisbane to make one of the net wickets an Indian-style turner and he'd bat on it all day for weeks, practising the techniques he'd learned at a 'spin camp' in Chennai in 1999, hosted by the legendary Bishan Bedi. The camp's motto was, 'When facing spin in India, you don't reach for the bouncing ball, you either take it on the full or wait.'

Australia would score 349 in its first innings, putting us 173 in front. Sadagoppan Ramesh and Rahul Dravid started well for India in their second dig, taking the score to 2 for 103. Then Dravid slapped a ball to Slater at square leg. Slater dived forward and claimed the catch, but it looked suss.

On television, Tony Greig spoke for many when he said, 'He's holding it up. Did he catch it? I don't think so. I thought that bounced. Well ... from here I thought it bounced.'

Dravid agreed and stood his ground while the dismissal was referred upstairs. As the third umpire studied the footage, Slater appeared to tell Dravid it was a fair catch and seemed offended that Dravid hadn't taken his word for it. When the decision came through that it was not out, a clearly emotional Slater got right in Dravid's face. Dravid held his gaze, silent. Unblinking. Dravid was called 'the Wall' because his defence was impenetrable, and it appeared his mind was too.

At the time, Slater had undiagnosed bipolar disorder, which manifested in late-night panic attacks, some of which resulted in him being rushed to hospital. But there was no one in the touring squad he could talk to about his mental health. There wasn't a team psychologist. And when Slater approached John Buchanan, he said the Australian coach, famous for his inspirational quotes and taking Steve Waugh to impromptu meetings with Edward de Bono, wasn't much help.

'When I needed someone to sit down and say "how are you doing?" he didn't offer me anything,' Slater told *The Guardian*. Adding to Slater's problems was that his marriage was breaking down and he'd also taken up smoking. I don't know why 'taking up smoking' is always mentioned as part of that trifecta. I guess the idea of taking up smoking in your 30s is shorthand for saying things aren't quite right.

Our bowlers were unaffected by the drama and limited India's second innings total to 219, leaving us 47 to win. Hayden and Slater guided Australia home without losing a wicket. One–nil. It was our 16th win in a row.

After play, it was Dravid who sought Slater out to resolve the issue of the claimed catch. The two of them had a long conversation and Slater's post-match mea culpa was moving.

'Sledging Rahul Dravid was one of the mistakes of my life,' Slater told reporters. 'He did not lose his cool even when I was hurling abuses at him. I could not stomach the fact that he was single-handedly demolishing the best team in the world. When the rage wore out on me, I realised that I was an animal and he was a gentleman. He won my heart instantly.'

Jimmy Barnes

In the late 90s/early 2000s, the profile writers who were offered the most work were the ones celebrities would confuse for shrinks. The result would be a quasi-therapy session that would be printed up on glossy paper and circulated to millions. That kind of journalism became my thing.

I like to think there was a bit of technique involved in encouraging celebrities to open up about their problems. First up, you can't have an agenda. If a celebrity thinks you want them to say something particular, then they'll clam shut. You need to have an open mind and an empathetic ear. I also found it helped to look as disorganised and unprepared as possible, which was easy for me as it was my natural state. If you had questions on separate bits of paper and your tape recorder looked like it had been thrown out a hotel window by Billy Idol, then they'd often do your job for you by telling you everything. I had the routine down pretty well by the time I met Jimmy

Barnes in the office of his record company in west Melbourne.

I wasn't a huge Barnesy fan. Obviously, I liked Chisel, but I wasn't quite in the demographic for his solo stuff. In early 2001, he wasn't the national treasure he is now. He wasn't raising people's spirits by singing songs with his family during a pandemic. Back then, he was the screaming boozer who helped Triple M listeners shed their anger. I liked my singers more angsty than that. But it turned out Barnesy was more angsty than any of them.

We sat on couches opposite each other. I put my tape recorder down in front of him and he soon started speaking in a stream of consciousness, like a husky Glaswegian David Helfgott. One thought spilled into the next ('That was great with Slater, I love him'). Sometimes he punched his right fist into his left hand ('You tell that reviewer mate of yours that I want a word with him'). Then he swore his life had been better since he met Deepak Chopra/started jogging/paid his outstanding tax bill/dyed his hair blond.

He told me about his childhood and how he was teased for not owning a school uniform. 'Couldn't afford uniforms. And they also gave me a hard time for having holes in my shoes. I'd have to put cardboard in the bottom of them. It was tough. Luckily, I didn't give a fuck. I had good fun. If anyone bagged me, I'd just belt 'em one. You don't forget shit like that just cos you've made some money. I know exactly where I came from.'

And then there was the fight with Chris Bailey from the Saints to win the heart of Jane Mahoney, the daughter of an Australian diplomat.

'I met her after a gig and I said, "Is this guy [Bailey] your boyfriend?" And she said, "No, no." But he was for a little while and so was I. We were both dating her. And every night, we'd both end up at her place at the same time. I would wait for him to leave and he'd be waiting for me to leave. Then, after about a month of this going on, I took him aside and threatened him. I said, "If you turn up again, I'm going to fucking kill ya." He never came back.

'I'm a pretty full-on person. I'm pretty wild. I like to have a good time. I party a lot. I'm not a fucking maniac, but I party. Mind you, I don't drink half as much as I used to. I used to drink a bottle of whisky and a bottle of Drambuie, straight. Then I'd go out partying. I was drinking three to four bottles of whisky a day. Then I changed to vodka because it got me pissed quicker.'

I liked Barnesy. Before the interview, I thought he'd be a bit of a tough guy, but he was as hurt and vulnerable as any other artist trying to make sense of the world. I told him I had to go because I was catching a plane to Stuttgart to interview AC/DC. He looked disappointed we couldn't chat longer, but he said to say 'hi' to the boys for him.

'It's not all about vodka anymore,' he said, getting up to shake my hand. 'It's all about balance, you see ... What does Deepak say ...? "You must do what you enjoy and employ the law of least effort." Basically, what he's saying is if you try too fucking hard, things don't work out well.'

It was obvious why Slater was drawn to Barnes: he saw someone similar to him. They were both intensely creative. Both liked to party. Both had forceful personalities that sometimes pissed people off. And they both ended up feeling increasingly isolated. In 2005, Slater revealed that he was already in the depths of unmanaged bipolar when he joined Barnes on stage at the Allan Border Medal while Barnes had contemplated taking his own life.

But because sporting careers are short, Slater had less time to resolve his issues.

Dravid and VVS

The Second Test started in Kolkata with Steve Waugh winning the toss, electing to bat, and Hayden (97), Slater (42) and Langer (58) bringing us to 1–193. Then Indian off spinner Harbhajan Singh started weaving his magic. His swagger and grin were annoyingly Australian. More frustrating was the fact that most of our guys had no idea how to play him. Harbhajan broke through with the wickets of Hayden and Mark Waugh. Then the 20-year-old got the first hat-trick in Indian Test history by claiming three future Hall of Famers in Ponting, Gilchrist and Warne. Australia slumped to 8 for 269. Steve Waugh (110) led a resurgence, partnering with Gillespie (46) then McGrath (22) to bring us to a potentially match-winning 445.

I had a sense of foreboding about Harbhajan, though. He'd played eight Tests as a teenager, been dropped, and was now back with the authority of a seasoned pro. The way he looked at the Australian batters, with a half-smile and a glint in his eye, showed he had it all over them. I could imagine him spooking us for eternity. But I put him out of my mind for a few hours when our bowlers rolled India for 171 and we appeared to be sailing to our 17th Test win.

Then Waugh enforced the follow-on. I don't remember it being a point of contention in the media, but I felt anxiety about it. If India were able to get more than 100 in front, I wasn't super confident of us getting the runs against Harbhajan on a crumbling deck.

At the end of Day 3, India were 4–232 in their second innings, trailing by just 42 with six wickets in hand. The Australians were almost certain to be chasing some sort of total, but there were no concerns about it in the dressing room. In fact, on the morning of Day 4, Steve Waugh was so confident, he placed a bottle of Southern Comfort under his chair for that night's celebrations. And then Michael Slater tempted fate even further when he produced a box of cigars, provocatively sniffed one and announced that 'Tonight's the night, boys. Tonight's the night.'

That day, we did not get a wicket.

Australian sporting teams are better in the role of underdog. As soon as they allow Icarus syndrome to take hold, everything backfires. Particularly in cricket. Greek mythology should be taught to every Australian cricketer before they're presented with their Baggy Green. There is a 100 per cent likelihood that the universe, or God, or gods will mock an Australian if they sniff a cigar in anticipation of victory.

What happened on Day 4 was that VVS Laxman and Rahul Dravid batted. And batted. And, despite the efforts of McGrath and Warne – arguably the greatest bowlers in history – they just never got out.

I went to work and they were still in. Came home – still in. I thought I was the problem and turned the radio off for an hour, hoping my absence would bring about a wicket. It didn't. I thought back to 1998 when a young Dravid took Waugh out to dinner after India's tour of Australia and quizzed him 'endlessly' about the mental side of cricket and how to take his own game to the next level. Waugh had his own generosity to blame as he stood in the searing Kolkata heat for the next 104 overs as Dravid and VVS took the game away from Australia – first slowly, then gleefully. They'd go on to share a 376-run stand for the fifth wicket and help set Australia a target of

384 to chase in little more than two sessions on Day 5. We began strongly thanks to a 74-run stand from Hayden and Slater, but capitulated at the hands of Harbhajan, who added six wickets to his seven in the first innings and finished Australia off in one of Test cricket's most famous defeats.

It was just the third time in Test history that a team lost a match after making the opposition follow-on, and Australia had been the losers on all three occasions. I couldn't see a path to victory for us in the Third Test. Harbhajan had spooked us. We were rattled.

AC/DC

I was starting to get really worried about Mum. I knew her doctor wasn't covering all bases. And that would stop me from sleeping. Whenever I did fall asleep, I'd wake up again within minutes, panicked that she was going to die. I couldn't imagine what she was going through, the pain and fear. Being an only child, of course I made it all about me. What was I going to do without her? Being aware of your own narcissism doesn't make it better. I was about to get on the plane to Germany for a week when Dad told me they were booked in to see a new oncologist in Albury. That was good. They were taking control of the situation.

I arrived at the hotel in Stuttgart after 26 hours in the air and AC/DC's publicist told me I had to interview the band straightaway. She added that any mention of former singer Bon Scott was strictly forbidden. Bon had died 21 years earlier from what a coroner called 'acute alcohol poisoning'. The topic was still raw, particularly for Malcolm Young. I nodded, reached for my notebook and crossed out my first five questions.

I was ushered into a conference room where Brian Johnson was making himself a coffee while Angus and Malcolm Young sat at the table, smoking and laughing. Angus was in the middle of an anecdote – and it was about Bon. I turned my tape recorder on.

Angus Young: 'He wouldn't let anyone touch me. I remember we were in St Louis one day. Don't know exactly when. It was our first time there and we were playing at a bar. At the end of the night, it turned into an all-in brawl. I mean, I'd been feeling really good cos my teeth had been fixed. Really good. And I'm smiling at everyone. Smilin' away. And suddenly, I see this fist comin' straight for my head. And Bon was behind me. And he just picked up whatever he could – chair or stool or something – and went *bang!* over this guy's head. And the guy went down. And Bon's standin' over him saying, "Hey mate, he just paid for them new choppers."'

There were laughs all round. Angus ashed in the tray again. He'd enjoyed telling the story and knew we'd enjoyed listening. Then his smile turned into a sad, mid-distance stare. Malcolm looked down. Brian stirred his coffee – it wasn't his place to break the silence.

Angus Young: 'Bon couldn't understand why I didn't drink. He'd look at me and laugh. He'd say, "How do you fucking do it? How's this bloke go on stage after a glass of milk?" He'd laugh. He thought it was hilarious. But he always said, "Whatever I do. Whatever I get up to. Don't follow."'

We talked for about half an hour. When the interview was over, I joined the other Australian journalist at the hotel bar for a beer. Brian came and joined us. What else was he going to do? We were all stuck in a hotel together in Stuttgart. A 6'1" German waitress approached and asked Brian if he'd like something to drink.

'Can I get a cup of coffee, wee darling?' he asked. And when she brought it, 'Thank you, my little angel.'

I asked if he still raced vintage cars. He said he did and it was going well, but added, 'Paul Newman beats me all the time even though he's 74 years of fucking age. He's quick, you know, very skilful.' Meanwhile, in a pair of chairs nearby, Angus and Malcolm drank milkshakes and called Philip Morris to complain there wasn't enough tar in the German Benson & Hedges. After beating up on the cigarette manufacturers Angus and Malcolm joined our conversation. I told them that Jimmy Barnes had said to say 'hello'. Angus nodded, but Malcolm looked lost for a moment.

'Swannee's brother,' said Angus. I'm sure it isn't often that Barnes is referred to as the brother of Adelaide singer John Swan, but the Young brothers walk to a different beat.

After dinner, one of AC/DC's roadies knocked on my hotel room door and said he and Brian were going in search of some medication to help Brian's ailing voice and did I want to come for a drive? I'd been in Germany seven hours and suddenly I was being seconded on a mission to save Brian Johnson's voice. I grabbed my jacket. Within minutes, I was sitting in the back of the German equivalent of a Tarago as it weaved its way through the streets of Stuttgart. Up the front, Brian and the roadie, who spoke in a thick Liverpudlian accent, were talking about Jimmy Page and how he'd lost a lot of weight.

Roadie: 'There was a time when Pagey put on a lot of weight, didn't he?'

Brian Johnson: 'Yep, but he's lost it now.'

R: 'That's right, he's lost it now.'

BJ: 'He put it on and then he took it off.'

R: 'Yep, he put it on, then took it off.'

We all sat in silence, contemplating how the guy who dressed like a wizard – and played guitar like one as well – put on a lot of weight, then took it off.

Brian said that Page was 'royalty'. He then talked about a certain rock star who wasn't royalty – a singer who'd hired legendary blues guitarist Donald 'Duck' Dunn to play in his touring band.

'They were playing some stadium and Duck's guitar string broke. And the little upstart said, "Where's your second guitar, you fucking idiot?" And Duck shot him a look, like this, you know?'

Brian turned around to demonstrate his version of a death stare.

'Like this. He looked at him and said, "If you must know, it went down with Otis." Yeah? Eh? The fucking upstart was able to see exactly where he stood as far as music royalty is concerned. Not that fucking high, I can tell you. Fucking cunt.'

The roadie pulled up at a shop that looked like a sort of deli, with dried meat hanging from the ceiling. I was told to stay in the car while they headed inside and talked to the shopkeeper. I watched as Brian pointed to his throat. Cash was exchanged. Brian was handed a package.

Next morning at breakfast, I asked Brian if the medication worked.

'Absolute shite. Did nothing for the voice. But you should see the size of my cock.'

That night, on stage in some stadium in Stuttgart, AC/DC wheeled out the hits one by one. There was 'Stiff Upper Lip', 'Hells Bells', 'You Shook Me All Night Long', 'TNT', 'Safe In New York City', 'Rock and Roll Ain't Noise Pollution' and of course '(She's Got) The Jack'. How the Germans loved The Jack. It was starting to get hot inside the venue and some fans were struggling to breathe. There was a lot of fainting and people being stretchered out, but nobody standing took their eyes off the band. Phil Carson, former chairman of Atlantic and the man who signed AC/DC to its first international deal, stood next to me as medics tended to the fans in front.

'It's hot,' said Phil. 'I really shouldn't have worn cashmere.'

After the gig, the other Australian journalist and I waited backstage for the band to finish their post-show post-mortem. We were going to congratulate them as if they were our friends. It'd be weird not to after hanging out with them, talking shit with them and going on excursions to procure secret potions. Then we realised the absurdity of what we were doing – they were AC/DC. And we were us. They didn't want to hang out with us. So we let them get on with their lives as rock stars while we got in a cab and headed to a pub called Wish You Were Beer.

Next morning, the phone rang. It was AC/DC's publicist. She asked what we got up to after the gig. I told her about Wish You Were Beer. She didn't laugh.

'What a shame. Cos Brian was looking for you. After the gig, he said, "Send in the Aussie boys. I want to see the Aussie boys." So I went looking for you and you weren't there. Shame.'

The last time I felt such regret was when Shania Twain asked me to join her for a post-interview lunch and I declined because I was on deadline. This was worse, though. I should have listened to Angus when he told me that 'In life you've gotta be prepared to take the plunge.'

I had to stop running away from 'the plunge'.

When I arrived back in Melbourne, the news was bad. Mum had received a second opinion from the oncologist in Albury, who'd immediately ordered an MRI. It showed she had secondary cancer in her bones that needed chemotherapy.

More pressing was the large cancer found on her femur that threatened to disintegrate the bone. Part of the femur would need to be removed and a steel rod inserted. I wanted to go to Wodonga to be by her side for the operation, but Dad didn't want to worry about me being on the road. He said he had enough to worry about. So from the moment Mum was wheeled into surgery at 8 am, I sat on my couch in my flat and waited. I didn't look at the computer, I didn't read, I didn't take phone calls, I didn't eat, drink or even breathe properly – I just waited. There was no way I could distract myself. I didn't want to do anything that would rock the universe one way or another. It was a monster surgery and I was concerned she wouldn't come out of it. Dad said he'd know how it had gone by about 3 pm and would give me a call. At 6.30 pm, the phone rang. The operation was successful. And by 'successful', Mum had survived. Now she had to recover, learn to walk again, and start radiation and chemotherapy.

Harbhajan

The deciding Test in Chennai started predictably enough with Waugh winning the toss. We batted. Hayden made 203. His strategy was straight out of Muhammad Ali's Rumble in the Jungle playbook – wear out the attack then dominate them. It didn't matter where the ball pitched, the big left-hander seemed to be able to sweep it. Mark Waugh backed him up with 70, and Steve Waugh looked like he was settling in for another century when he attempted a sweep and was struck on the pad. Harbhajan appealed and the broadcast immediately cut to the umpire shaking his head. Meanwhile, off screen, while Waugh had eyes on the umpire, the ball had lobbed in the air, bounced and was spinning back toward the stumps. From the non-striker's end Hayden yelled, 'Look out, Tugga', and Waugh instinctively palmed the ball away from the stumps, which resulted in the Australian captain being only the sixth cricketer in Test history to be out handling the ball. It was a free wicket to India. What followed was another capitulation at the hands of Harbhajan. Australia lost the next 7 wickets for 51 runs.

What Harbhajan did to Ponting almost broke my heart. He made one of the greatest batters in the world look like he was drunk. Ponting didn't know whether to go forward or back to the off spinner and his hesitancy crippled him. Australia was all out for 391, with Harbhajan taking seven wickets.

We could have done with 60 more, but 391 was probably enough to keep us competitive. But then Tendulkar, who hadn't scored a century in the series, corrected that anomaly with a robust 126, and Laxman (65) and Dravid (81) continued their form to lift India to 501, 110 runs in front of Australia. Australia's response of 264 was not quite enough. Resistance to Harbhajan came in the form of Slater (48), Mark Waugh (57) and Steve Waugh (47), but they all ended up falling to the off spinner, who picked up eight wickets, taking his match tally to 15.

India started chasing the target of 155 confidently enough, getting to 1 for 76. Then Colin Miller, who had been drafted for the final Test, picked up Dravid and Laxman and India were suddenly 7–135, 20 short of a series win. Fast bowler Zaheer Khan then combined with keeper Sameer Dighe to put on 16 runs before McGrath picked up Zaheer and Harbhajan made his way to the crease with eight wickets down and four runs to get. Harbhajan held his nerve and appropriately scored the winning runs.

The influence Harbhajan had on this series wasn't something that could ever have been anticipated. He stymied Steve Waugh's last stand in India – the place he'd worked so hard to embrace with an eye to conquering. Waugh called it 'The Final Frontier'. And so it remained.

CHAPTER 9

2001 Ashes Tour of England

'Cricket is battle and service and sport and art.'

– Douglas Jardine

Australia could have been adrift after the loss in India. Instead, the team used defeat as motivation. Waugh was clear about his ambitions at the start of the Ashes tour, saying, 'If we can get on top of England early, we can open some old scars.'

First, he had to open some scars in his own line-up, namely those of his close mate Justin Langer.

Langer hadn't had a bad tour of India, averaging more than Ponting, Gilchrist and Mark Waugh, and fully expected to continue his role as Australia's number three. But two days before the First Test, Steve Waugh knocked on his door and told him he wouldn't be playing.

'This is my hero and my big brother, telling me that I was out and I was literally shocked, I just didn't see it coming,' Langer told *Wisden*. 'I didn't know whether to cry on his shoulder or punch him out.'

Langer felt persecuted. He was 30 years old and had been in and out of the Test side since he was 22, never properly cementing a spot, and it felt like his last chance had just been taken from him.

The late commentator Peter Roebuck wrote that in the Australian Cricket Academy's class of 1990, 'Shane Warne was the talented rogue. Damien Martyn was the arrogant gun. Greg Blewett was the cheerful local. Langer was the mad toughie who spent most of his time climbing ropes, punching bags and hitting cricket balls. No one thought he'd reach the big time.'

Adam Gilchrist played against Langer in his late teens and told the *Sydney Morning Herald* that he was 'short in stature, really defensive left-handed batsman who could hardly hit the ball off the pitch. He didn't look like the most talented batsman around, I can tell you.'

I understood Langer. I'd been the guy who thought he had something to offer when most people were unconvinced. You become so desperate to prove yourself that you do the jobs no one else wants. For me, it was interviewing the editor's favourite Australian band, The Masters Apprentices, on 11 separate occasions. For Langer, it was debuting at number three in the Fourth Test against the West Indies in 1993, when Curtly Ambrose and Courtney Walsh were at their zenith. Number three was the position for the best batter in the team, not the debutant. But no one wanted to face the West Indies when the ball was still new. So Allan Border asked Langer if he'd be willing to do it and Langer said, 'No worries, AB. I would love to.' 'Love' is a strong word for the role he was about to undertake. But this was a guy who wore his new Baggy Green to bed the night before the Test.

When Mark Taylor got out fourth ball, Langer only had one pad on. When he finally made his way out there, the third ball he faced from Ian Bishop crashed into his helmet. It was a wicked blow and probably concussed him, but there were no tests for concussion in those days. From the commentary box, Bill Lawry stated the obvious: 'That's a bit of a nasty one. Certainly stopped him. He's not sure where he is. He's in a bit of trouble.' David Boon, watching from the non-striker's end, suggested Langer retire hurt, telling him there are 'no heroes in Test cricket'.

Langer declined – he wasn't going to give up his chance. He'd go on to be hit on the body five more times in the next seven overs. Langer made 20 in Australia's first innings and then a gutsy half century in the second. In the final Test at the WACA, he scored 10 and 1. As a response to his two failures, he hung a sign in his shower that said *The pain of discipline is nothing like the pain of disappointment.*

Langer was in and out of the team for the next seven years. It was a career of failures, multiple blows to the head, affirmations and gutsy resurrections. Ultimately, he was seen as a slow-scoring battler and by the 2001 Ashes, he'd played 41 Tests with an average just under 40. And here he was being dropped again.

After Waugh left his hotel room, Langer resolved to make an undeniable case to get back in the side by crushing it in tour games against counties. That didn't happen; he averaged less than 20. He later blamed his lacklustre performances on wanting to succeed too much.

'I believe in the ethos, "The harder you try, the worse it gets",' he said. 'Particularly as an athlete because you tighten up ... I couldn't be batting any worse, I wasn't making any runs, and I was getting angrier and angrier and more desperate because the dream was going.'

Free for Free

I hadn't had an audition in almost a year. It wasn't like I'd given up on acting; it just seemed acting had given up on me. And I was comfortable with that. I was going to be a filmmaker anyway. I just needed to get around to making a film. Then, out of the blue, I was asked to audition for a health insurance ad. It was to play a guy with comically protruding front teeth. He goes into a health insurance office and asks for their promoted deal of three months' health insurance for free – which was called 'Three for Free' – but because of his buck teeth, he asks for '*Free* for free'. I put the script down and thought that whoever does this is opening themselves up to public humiliation on a grand scale and there was no way I'd be going anywhere near it. Twenty-four hours later, I was sitting in a casting agent's waiting room with a bunch of other 20-something men. We'd all had the same idea of buying teeth lollies to insert into our mouths for the duration of the audition.

I did the scene a couple of times in front of the director, producer and client. They seemed pleased. I only half wanted the job, which always made me better in the audition room. On the way out, I got a call from Dad. Mum had had another MRI and they found a cancer tumour on her liver and she needed more chemotherapy. He passed the phone to Mum, who remained upbeat for my benefit. She didn't want to talk about her condition. She just wanted to know what I was up to.

I couldn't speak. 'It's OK,' she said. 'I'm just a bit crook. I'll get better.' I felt ashamed that she had to comfort me.

Dad came back on the phone and said the doctor was confident she could reduce the size of the tumour.

'But what about getting rid of it?' I asked.

'I don't think she can get rid of it,' Dad said. 'But she can reduce it.'

He said that when Mum was well enough, they'd go on a long holiday. At that time, Dad's only solace was walking the circumference of the Beechworth golf course, reciting the Lord's Prayer over and over. I put the phone down. Cortisol had already been released into my bloodstream. I was so stressed, I was numb.

The phone rang again. This time, it was my agent.

I was the 'Free for Free' guy.

When I woke up at 4.30 on the morning of the Free for Free ad, I could hear Mike, the guy upstairs, rattling around above me. He was 6'4", covered in tatts and drove trucks. I liked him because he made sure no one in the block of apartments played loud music. If they did, they were quickly told to 'TURN THAT SHIT DOWN!' And if a party went beyond 10 pm, he'd knock on their door and shout: 'PARTY'S OVER, FUCKERS.' When a nice couple moved in downstairs with their crying baby, he had no problem yelling repeatedly: 'GIVE THE KID A DUMMY!!!' Mike was an insomniac, though, so he couldn't take advantage of all the silence he created. I left at 5 am, shutting the front door a little hard on exit. Mike was on to it straightaway. 'DON'T SLAM THE FUCKING DOOR.'

I must've been tired and cranky and not quite in charge of my faculties because I yelled back, 'IT WAS A FUCKING ACCIDENT.'

Mike bounded down the stairs after me. My first instinct was to run because I wanted to protect my face for the ad. Then I remembered he lived above me and could beat me up any time he liked. Possibly several times a day. So I stopped jumping down the stairs five at a time, turned and faced him. 'Mike, I'm sorry. I've been going through a rough patch. It was never my intention to speak coarsely to you. Please accept my apology.'

He crunched his eyes shut, lowered his clenched fists to his sides and let out a long, frustrated growl. He really wanted to take my head off, but he was a gentleman, and an apology was an apology.

On set, I was ushered into the make-up area, where the fake teeth were glued into my mouth before I had a chance to eat breakfast. I'm not great on an empty stomach. But I told myself that it was just one day. From make-up I was taken onto the set, which had been pre-lit, and we launched straight into the scene.

AZ: 'Yeah, I'd like to get Free for Free.'

Receptionist: 'Sorry?'

AZ: 'I wanna get Free for Free.'

Receptionist: 'I'm sorry, what for "free"?'

AZ: 'I want ... to get ... free ... for free.'

Reception: '*Three* for free?'

AZ: 'Free for free, that's it.'

We didn't get much filmed in the morning because the light wasn't right, or the camera was in the wrong place or the background wasn't 'popping'. As lunch approached, we started to smell roast chicken coming from the caterer's truck. Already strung out because of my lack of breakfast, the aroma from the caterer's truck was tormenting me to the point that I was dreaming about lunch while Cindy, 'the receptionist', was saying her lines. Maybe they'd have a pavlova for dessert. But as we walked up to the dining area, the make-up department told me I couldn't eat because it would take too much time to unglue the fake teeth then glue them back in again.

'Whaaaa?!'

'I know. Sorry Adam. You're doing a really great job!'

At lunch, well-meaning crew kept coming up to me while shoving pavlova into their mouths and asking if they were my real teeth. I'd say they weren't. And they'd say, 'Are you sure? Ha ha.'

We started again after lunch and by 7 pm we'd done the perfect take. The performances, the light and the background all sang. They checked the film gate for any debris that might've scratched the film stock and spoiled the shot and it was clear. Everyone cheered. Most of all, me, because I really needed food. But when they played the footage back, they saw a boom mic quietly creeping into shot. It had been 22 hours since food had passed my lips and I tried to show my frustration. The teeth stopped me from articulating properly, and everyone just thought I was making funny noises and waving my arms around to lighten the mood.

We got it in the can by around eight o'clock.

That night, I walked up the stairs to my flat to find three cops lurking outside. One of them asked if this was Mike's flat. I said it wasn't and quietly pointed them to the flat directly above me.

They knocked on his door loudly. Too loudly. Mike would've hated it.

Cop 1: 'Come on, Mike. We know you're in there, big fella.'

Cop 2: 'Get your toothbrush, buddy. You're going to be going away for a little while.'

As a handcuffed Mike was led down the stairs, he shot me a rueful grin. I was disappointed to see him leave. Without him, the whole apartment block would go to the dogs. And I could have done with him when the ad came out and I suddenly became 'popular'. To be clear, this wasn't sexy Hemsworth-style popularity. It was people-waiting-outside-my-door-with-cupcakes popularity. They knew my address because it was in the phone book, and they knew how to find my unit in the difficult-to-navigate apartment complex because the manager of the property obligingly told them. Mike would have taken care of all that. Damn you, Mike, and whatever you did.

The cops placed a careful hand on the top of Mike's head as he lowered himself into the police car. Meanwhile, the baby downstairs cried with abandon.

The First, Second and Third Tests

Australia won the First Test against England by an innings and 188 runs thanks to centuries from Gilchrist (152), Steve Waugh (105) and Damien

Martyn (105), who quickly justified his selection in place of Langer. After the Test, Waugh decided to take the team to Wimbledon to support Pat Rafter against the fast-serving Goran Ivanisevic in the Men's Final. Before they left, he told the team he thought it would be cool if they all wore their Baggy Green caps to show solidarity with Rafter. Langer, McGrath, Gilchrist and Hayden were all for it. Shane Warne wasn't. Warne told BBC Radio that he thought the idea was 'embarrassing' and that the captain was fetishising the cap. 'I looked at Mark Waugh and he said, "I'm not wearing it", and I said, "I'm not wearing it either." To think that these grown men wore green baggy caps to Wimbledon! So I refused,' Warne said. 'Looking back at some of those photos ... it was embarrassing to watch.'

The differences in opinion regarding the Baggy Green didn't hurt Australia's performance in the Second Test, which we won by eight wickets on the back of five-wicket hauls from McGrath and Gillespie and a majestic 108 from Mark Waugh.

Two–nil to Australia.

Ten days before the Third Test, in which Australia would try to win the Ashes for a record seventh series in a row, Steve Waugh played squash with world number one Sarah Fitz-Gerald. It was meant to be no more than a photo opportunity to promote the 2002 Commonwealth Games in Manchester, but Waugh had played as a kid and wanted to impress.

'We played for 10 or 20 minutes and then got really competitive,' he told *The Age*. 'She's obviously a great player. I ran around like a lunatic for a couple of hours.'

After the game, Waugh noticed he'd pulled up tight in the back of his calves, but immediately put it out of his mind.

In the Third Test, England won the toss, batted, and were skittled for 185 with McGrath picking up 5 for 49. It was a tricky pitch and Australia collapsed to 8–122. Adam Gilchrist then blasted ten fours in his 54 and Gillespie hung on for 27, bringing Australia to 190 and putting us five runs in front. The England second innings started well thanks to Marcus Trescothick (32) and Mike Atherton (51), but soon collapsed to be all out for 162, courtesy of Warne's 6–33. We were set 158 runs to win, which we made short work of. The only hiccup in the Australian innings was when Steve Waugh called his brother Mark through for a sharp single and tore the calf he'd strained playing squash. So at the exact moment Australia won the Test and retained the Ashes, a miserable-looking Steve Waugh was in a wheelchair at a Nottingham hospital, watching it on television. He had two tears in his calf – one 5 cm, the other 2 cm. Doctors told him he'd be out for four to six months. Waugh called his wife, Lynette, and told her he'd be coming home as there was no point in him staying, but Lynette insisted he stay so he could collect the Ashes trophy on the balcony at The Oval after the final Test.

That's when Waugh and team physiotherapist Errol Alcott decided to try to produce a miracle to get him fit for the Fifth Test, only 19 days away. Alcott would spend ten hours a day with Waugh, five of which were dedicated to massaging the captain's damaged calf to realign the frayed muscle fibres. The rest of the time, Alcott would oversee the Australian captain's stretching, walking, swimming and gym sessions.

Meanwhile, Langer sensed opportunity in Waugh's injury. He believed he was the man to replace the skipper in the Fourth Test. All he needed to do was impress in the tour game against Sussex. In the first innings at Hove, Langer batted with Gilchrist, who was handling the bowling with ease, hitting to all parts of the ground. Meanwhile, Langer struggled to hit the ball past the playing square before capitulating for two. He remained optimistic and was determined to put a big score together in the second dig. When he was out for 14, he took out his frustrations on Gilchrist, the stand-in captain and a tour selector, grabbing him and pinning him up against the dressing room wall and yelling, 'Look what you blokes have done to me!'

Coach John Buchanan told the *Sydney Morning Herald* that he remembered Langer, still hurt after being dumped at the start of the series, telling Gilchrist, 'You betrayed me!' and 'You ripped my heart out!'

Simon Katich was preferred to Langer in the Fourth Test, and Langer told his wife he was going to retire.

She took his words seriously enough to fly over to be with him in case he did. That sleepy tour match against Sussex when Langer physically and verbally assaulted one of his best mates could have been his Waterloo, but it could also just have been a nasty bump in the road. It would depend entirely on luck.

Wilfred

I'd built up enough savings by now to make my first short film. It was a period piece based on the true story of a Melbourne journalist who'd had an affair with Ava Gardner when she was making *On the Beach* in 1951. In my film, the journalist also strikes up a friendship with Ava's co-star, Gregory Peck, and comes to blows with Frank Sinatra. I cast myself as the journalist and we filmed over several weekends on a Hi8 camcorder I'd bought at Myer. Apart from the script, my performance and the camcorder, the biggest problem was continuity. Ava's cigarettes would expand and shrivel in the space of a breath and in one scene I grew a moustache in the time it took to walk from the bathroom to the kitchen.

The role of making sense of the rushes fell to an editor called Carlo, who I didn't know but had come recommended. Our working relationship started when I turned up to a South Melbourne post-production facility at the appointed time and was led into a room where Carlo sat in front of a large computer. Carlo looked like a young Gene Simmons – his hair was black and long with a streak of blond running down one side.

AZ: 'Hi. I'm Adam.'

Silence.

AZ: 'Tim said you were a bit of a genius, I think you might need to be with the footage I shot. Ha ha.'

Silence.

AZ: 'What are you editing on, Avid or Final Cut?'

Silence.

Carlo wasn't for talking and I wasn't paying him enough to force words to come out of his mouth. So I moved to the back of the room and picked up a magazine. Five minutes went by before Carlo spoke his first words.

Carlo: 'Had a threesome last night.'

Not even a guy who'd had a threesome the previous night could fix this film. Carlo motioned to the screen and asked who the Irishman was. I said it was Gregory Peck. Later, he wondered why Ava was interested in 'him'. And when he said 'him', he pointed to an image of me. Not even turning the film black and white and adding a jazz score we didn't have the rights to could render it watchable.

I felt like a failure. I knew what a good film was, but instead of working out where I'd gone wrong and how I could do better next time, I threw my toys out of the pram. I resolved that I had no aptitude for filmmaking and my life-calling was obviously interviewing actors and rock stars.

Then, despite my misgivings, I made two more films. They were better. Still not good. But better. They both starred Jason Gann, who, by this stage, was carving out a solid career in Brisbane theatre.

Jason was on his way to Melbourne to stay at my place for a few weeks so we could make a short film in which he'd play a faded rock star who'd fallen on hard times. When he walked in the door, he looked the best he'd ever looked. He was tanned and in good shape, but it was his hair that stood out. It'd be too much to say he looked like Brad Pitt in *Spy Game* – but at that moment, his *hair* definitely looked like Brad Pitt's hair did in *Spy Game*.

'I went to a hair *styyylist*,' he said. 'She didn't want to be called a hairdresser. She said she was a *stylist*.'

Jason's stylist was a genius. His hair would later be 'styled' by the best Hollywood had to offer, but no subsequent styling would ever lay a finger on this masterpiece. It was perfect for the faded rocker character. But before we could start on that, Jason was going to country Victoria for a couple of days to play the small role of a Nazi in an independent feature.

While he was away, I was invited to a party, met a woman and went back to her place, where I made friends with her dog. The woman made us a cup of tea while I threw a ball to her dog and he caught it. We did this multiple times and there were a lot of pats. The woman said the dog liked me. 'That's a good sign,' she said. 'He doesn't like all my friends.'

A little bit later, the woman and I moved to the bedroom. The dog joined us, and this was when the dog's attitude changed. He sat at the end of the bed and stared at me with cold, unblinking eyes. I knew he was trying to communicate something to me and I imagined it to be along the lines of, 'What do you think you're gonna do to my missus?'

The dog was not happy. I wasn't happy either. The woman thought the situation was hilarious. I explained I was feeling emotionally fragile and that I might go home. The woman didn't offer to get the dog off the bed. She just nodded and said, 'Goodbye.' The whole thing was a test, and I'd failed.

I got dressed and the dog enthusiastically jumped off the bed and escorted me to the door. 'Going so soon, Adam? Didn't even get a chance to naughty boy her? What a shame. See ya, Adam.'

Next day, I spoke to Jason on the phone. He was on his way back from the 'film', which sounded like a ruse to get a group of young actors to take their shirts off in front of a camera and play Nazis. I encouraged him to get back here so we could start on our own film. And he was like, 'Yeeeah ... we need to talk about that.'

Jason turned up at my flat and it was immediately clear there would be no faded rocker film. The hair that had been so beautifully crafted was now shaved to the skin at the back and sides, leaving just a tuft at the top. And that tuft had been dyed black. His hair had gone from Brad Pitt to Kim Jong-un. Jason was inconsolable, and also had a pimple in his nostril.

We sat in my living room, both of us going through our own hell, when I mentioned the woman and her dog. Jason and I had spent hundreds of hours improvising characters over the years and immediately slipped into him being the dog and me being me. It was funnier than our usual improvisations, and within 20 minutes we were writing another short film. It was about a dog called Wilfred, who does his best to freak out his owner's date. I had a feeling we were on to something and that our lives were about to change. Which was silly. It was just a short film.

Next morning, I roped in Tony Rogers, who had made the 'Three for Free' ad, to direct, then hired $300,000 worth of camera equipment and bought a bunch of film offcuts from a guy at Kodak. The Kodak guy pulled up in his Fairlane. I handed him $1000 in cash and he handed me a bunch of film. We auditioned three actresses to play 'Sarah', but Cindy from the 'Three for Free' ad was always going to get it. She shared our humour and deadpanned at an elite level.

A week before the shoot, there was a drama with the dog suit. Tony didn't like the one we had, so we found a new one which Tony liked, but Jason hated. So Jason and I visited an old costume warehouse in Moonee Ponds which had one dog costume left. After peeling back the layers of bear and lion costumes, we finally found Wilfred. God knows how long he'd been hanging there just waiting for someone to wear him. He was saggy and ungainly and was probably last worn to a party in the late 70s. I couldn't imagine the wearer having a great night.

Tony swung by in his Alfa Romeo and fell in love with him too.

We shot the film over two days and I would've spent about $4500 renting camera, lights and sound equipment. I didn't take out insurance on any of it and, according to Jason, who was sleeping among the gear crammed into my living room, I'd wake him up most nights sleep-yelling at imaginary burglars trying to break into my flat. I was vulnerable at the time. So was Jason. I guess that gave a truth to our performances. And Tony's visual style brought an appropriate sense of menace. After the shoot, Jason went home to Brisbane while Tony and I cut the film over Christmas.

I decided that this would be my last go at breaking into the film industry. I couldn't do it to myself anymore. I'd spent nearly $20,000 trying to get my foot in the door and after this, I was done. I was about to turn 30 and I couldn't keep throwing cash on the fire.

We finished the edit and sent the film to Jason. He hated it. Then we sent it off to Tropfest, Australia's biggest short film competition. Maybe Jason was right. I didn't know if it was any good. All I knew was

I'd been through every millimetre of coverage and this was the best version of what we'd shot.

A few days later, there was an article in *The Age* saying there were 611 entries into Tropfest, a record. Two weeks went by before we discovered we'd made the shortlist of 60. Two weeks after that, I got two calls, one to say we'd made it into Tropfest's final 12, which would be screened in February in front of 100,000 people at Sydney's Domain.

The other was from Dad. Mum had been taken to hospital.

The Fourth and Fifth Tests

For the Fourth Test, Gilchrist replaced the injured Waugh as captain, won the toss and batted first. Ponting (144) and Martyn (118) starred in Australia's total of 447. McGrath's mighty seven wickets restricted England to 309. Then Australia declared in the second innings at 4–176, leaving England 315 to win.

I'm only marginally comfortable when Australia declares leaving the opposition a target of over 400. Leaving them a target of less than 350 makes my chest tighten and forces all the blood from my head. But a target of 315 meant that just one person needed to bat well and another satisfactorily, and it would be all over for Australia. And so it came to pass. Mark Butcher's 173 was complemented by returning skipper Nasser Hussain's 55 and England coasted to a six-wicket win.

Still, it'd been a good Ashes for Australia. We were up 3–1 going into the final Test. The batters were scoring runs, with Mark Waugh and Damien Martyn averaging 86 and 76 respectively. If there was a problem, it was Slater. After his breezy 77 off 82 balls in the First Test, he'd struggled. And by the end of the Fourth Test, his average for the tour had dropped to 24. According to Steve Waugh, the problem was his footwork.

'Slats was permanently on the move at the crease, which caused his balance to be poor and his head position to be exaggerated and loose,' wrote Waugh in *Out of My Comfort Zone*, '... [T]he longer this series went on the more he was "going fishing" outside off stump, a dead giveaway of poor form.'

Michael Slater was a revelation when he debuted for Australia on the Ashes tour of England in 1993. At the time, I didn't know it was possible for Australian openers to be that swashbuckling. I was used to Wood, Dyson, Laird, Wessels, Geoff Marsh, and Taylor. Their job was to take the shine off the new ball and they did it with grim-faced seriousness.

Then Slater came onto the scene, and instead of defending and leaving, he just hit balls that deserved to be hit. It didn't matter whether it was the first ball of a new series or the last before lunch – he never pulled his punches. When he scored his maiden century in his second Test at Lord's, he kissed the Australian crest on his helmet. And that became his thing.

This brash kid from Wagga Wagga, whose hair hung in there way after I predicted it would go, went on to make 14 centuries in his 74 Tests at 42.84. He also made nine scores in the 90s. As Gideon Haigh once wrote, 'He kept Matthew Hayden out of the team; what else can be said?'

In those days, mental health problems in sporting circles weren't handled with care, and Slater's undiagnosed bipolar disorder led his teammates to think he was unpredictable.

Before the series in India, Shane Warne and Victorian wicketkeeper Darren Berry had welcomed the NSW opener to the crease during a Shield match by intimating he was a time bomb.

Warne: 'Tick.'

Berry: 'Tock.'

Warne: 'Tick.'

Berry: 'Tock.'

The tag-team verbals between Warne and Berry continued until Slater holed out to deep mid wicket. Before he walked off, Slater glared at Warne and Berry, who yelled in unison: 'KABOOM!'

Not long after that came the altercation with Dravid in Mumbai, then an Ashes tour in which he'd gone out drinking alone, been disciplined for missing the team bus, and had performed below expectations. To further complicate matters, Slater's estranged wife, Stephanie, had come to England to try to reconcile their marriage. 'But that's impossible on tour,' Slater told *The Guardian*. 'It all ended in tears during the Fourth Test.'

On the eve of the Fifth Test, Waugh and Gilchrist decided it was time for Slater to be given 'a break' and believed Langer would do 'a great job' in his stead. It was difficult for them to get chairman of selectors Trevor Hohns on the same page. Hohns pushed hard for a stay of execution for Slater and made the point that they'd only picked two specialist openers for the tour. Waugh countered strongly with, 'You aren't here! The change needs to happen and it should be now.' Hohns was outvoted.

The following morning, Waugh, along with team manager Steve Bernard, told Slater the bad news. Slater's response was to tell them to 'go and get fucked'.

When Waugh announced the omission of Slater to the team at a training session, Slater heckled him. Gilchrist told Slater to shut up. Langer tried to calm everything down by making a heartfelt speech about what the Baggy Green should mean to all of them. Slater didn't complete the session, going back to his hotel room, where he was consoled by Hayden and Warne. He would never play Test cricket again.

After that, Langer seemed to inherit Slater's daring. He'd gone from being someone who looked like he was just trying to survive, to an assertive, fast-scoring showman. He scored 102 in the Fifth Test, alongside Mark Waugh's 120 and Steve Waugh's 157. Warne would get 11 wickets and Australia would win by an innings and 25 runs. Series over. Australia 4–1.

In his next 64 Tests, Langer made over 5000 runs at 49 with 16 hundreds. And his opening partnerships with Hayden averaged 51. It would be overstating it to say Langer had turned into a swan, but he had transitioned from an awkward-looking duckling to an extremely watchable duckling. And his affirmations, once ridiculed, suddenly took on greater meaning.

Talent never loses its voice, but sometimes, it is silent.

A friend once told me that "worry is like a rocking chair: you go backwards and forwards and nowhere".

Fast forward 15 years and Langer's the coach of the Australian men's team, having taken over from Darren Lehmann, whose favourite affirmation was *WTBC* ('Watch the ball, cunt').

Mum

Mum conquered the bone cancer, learned to walk again, and then had chemo to reduce the tumour on her liver.

Then, somewhere between the Lord's and Nottingham tests, Dad walked into their bedroom to find her quietly patting the mattress. He asked her what she was doing and she said, 'Nothing.'

When Mum and Dad had moved from Cairns to Beechworth, they'd built a beautiful house to Mum's specifications. Mum said that this was to be her final home. 'They're going to have to carry me out feet first, Boysie.' She called me Boysie. She'd say, 'Just go for it, Boysie', 'We're on your side, Boysie.' And, most optimistically of all, 'Your hair's looking good, Boysie.'

When Dad took her to hospital after finding her, momentarily, in that different state of consciousness, neither of them knew she'd be leaving home for the last time. The oncologist ran some scans of Mum's brain and didn't see anything that looked like cancer, but she wanted to do a lumbar tap, just to be sure.

While we waited for the results, Mum sat up in her hospital bed, helping me learn my lines for a guest stint on *SeaChange*. She'd always helped me with my lines. This time, there was a bit of a delay between me saying my line and her saying her line. This was unusual, because she'd always been fast at picking up cues.

AZ: 'Are you sure you want me to do the job, Mum?'

Mum: 'You have to do it, Boysie.'

When the pathology tests came back, the results were bad. There were cancer cells in the spinal fluid and almost certainly the sheath of her brain. Dad went home and packed a bag for her.

I divided my time between the *SeaChange* set in Williamstown, and Wodonga, where Mum was in hospital. One afternoon, I arrived at the hospital in time to hear Mum's oncologist say that there was nothing more they could do for her. The oncologist was upset – she was fond of Mum and wanted to know if Mum understood what she had just said. Mum shook her head. Her condition had become much worse and she was in a kind of dream. I was sitting in a chair at the end of her bed, paralysed by the scene in front of me. Dad and the oncologist took their discussion into the hospital corridor. I turned back to Mum and saw tears running down her cheeks.

Before she slipped into unconsciousness, Mum's last words to me were 'I love you very much, Boysie.' She was crying. I said I loved her as well.

I left the hospital to take Dad home, feeling that maybe this was the last time Mum and I would speak. Then I remembered I'd left my phone in her room. When I went back, she'd stopped crying and was delighted to see me. 'Hello Boysie,' she said, as if the previous interaction had never happened. The nurse asked her how she was feeling, and she said, 'I'm still here.'

We finished filming my *SeaChange* scenes on a Tuesday and Mum held on until I was able to return to Wodonga on the Wednesday morning. When I arrived, she was in a morphine-induced coma. I sat by her bed, held her hand, brushed her hair, read articles about food to her, because that was her passion.

Whenever there were long gaps in her breathing, I squeezed her hand – I couldn't let her die. And I'm so sorry for that.

That night, I took Dad home so he could get a couple of hours' sleep. I couldn't sleep, so I sat at the computer and started writing a long overdue story for the paper. While I was writing, I lost some time. It was as though I was in a deep meditation.

The phone rang at 9.30 pm. It was one of the nurses from the hospital saying that Mum had passed away. She'd just turned 60.

I went into Dad's room and told him. She was at peace, but my poor dad ... he just sat up in bed, a look of grief and distress across his face.

He told me to pray for her soul.

CHAPTER 10

2002–3 Ashes in Australia

'We don't play this game for fun.'

– Wilfred Rhodes

In early November 2002, as the Australian team prepared for the 2002–3 Ashes series, Steve Waugh had a feeling the selectors wanted the series to be his last. I had a feeling too. Possibly, the whole of Australia did.

The rot had set in eight months earlier when the selectors, headed by Trevor Hohns, dropped Steve Waugh as Australia's one-day captain. Hohns had been sensitive about exactly where to let Waugh know he'd been axed. He thought it would be a little harsh to give him the bad news in his hotel room on the day of the 2002 Allan Border Medal. So he had tried to do the deed the day before in Devonport, as Waugh waited to go in to bat for NSW in a limited-overs clash against Tasmania. Hohns asked the padded-up

Waugh for five minutes of his time. Waugh explained he was next in. A disappointed Hohns suggested they catch up in Melbourne the next day.

As Hohns made his way to Waugh's Melbourne hotel room on that February morning, Allan Border admitted to feeling physically ill. He was on the selection panel and knew what was about to happen. Australia had missed out on the final of the 2001–2 World Series Cup Tri-series versus South Africa and New Zealand and the selection panel was unanimous in its decision that Waugh had to go.

Hohns sat down and asked what he wanted to talk about first, Tests or one-dayers. Waugh said, 'Tests', and that part of the conversation was straightforward, as Waugh's test spot wasn't under immediate threat. Then Hohns moved to the one-dayers and told Waugh that the selectors didn't think he was one of the top six one-day batters in the country. Hard to believe they were referring to the same man who, just two years earlier in the '99 World Cup, mounted the greatest rearguard effort in the history of limited-overs cricket.

The decision was final. Waugh had played 325 One Day Internationals over 16 years. As captain, he'd taken Australia from seventh to first in the one-day rankings. And now his white ball career was over.

Waugh would later say he was 'stung' by the clinical efficiency of his sacking. The media coverage that followed was so extensive that Waugh's six-year-old daughter, Rosie, started calling her father 'Steve Waugh'.

I met Steve Waugh once. It was after I'd finished a performance of a play in Brisbane and had joined some mates at a nightclub overlooking the river. There among the heaving 90s throng was the Australian men's cricket team having their final get-together before leaving for the '96 World Cup. Damien Fleming was at the bar. Ricky Ponting left early with a grumpy look on his face. I stood at the urinal between Paul Reiffel and Michael Slater. Then, as I walked back into the club, I saw Steve Waugh having a quiet drink with some support staff. I introduced myself and he couldn't have been more decent. I had several questions I wanted to ask – why was his first nickname 'Drobe' and how did he transition to 'Tugga'? Why does he talk to himself while he bats? And when he first saw a cricket protector at the age of seven, was it true he tried to put it on his knee? But I refrained. I just wished him luck and made an uncharacteristically dignified exit. When I got home and looked in the mirror, I saw that in my rush to leave the theatre, I'd forgotten to take off my make-up. It wasn't white restoration make-up, but there was a substantial amount of base, eyeliner and rouge. Make-up on men was not a thing in those days. Well, not in Brisbane. And certainly not when talking to the Australian men's cricket team. So kudos to Waugh et al; they had every reason to take the piss, given the era and the hyper-masculinity of their workplace, but were decent enough not to.

In Waugh's first 52 Tests, he was a classy stroke player and clever medium pacer with a lot of promise, averaging mid-30s with the bat and more than 45 with the ball. But he was effective in One Day Internationals, back when there wasn't much separation in personnel between one-dayers and Tests. If you played well in a one-dayer, the selectors assumed you'd carry that form over to the five-day game and vice versa.

Waugh was dropped from the Test side for his brother Mark after a bad run in 1991. He was then recalled for the tour of the Caribbean later that year before being dropped again after two Tests. He returned for the 1992–93 Australian summer, but his form was patchy and he heard he was about to be dropped again. So he immediately walked out and made 100. It would herald the beginning of Waugh's habit of being great when the chips were down. Australians liked that. It reminded them of Border. We also liked that he'd made sacrifices with his stroke selection by deleting the more risky hook and pull from his repertoire.

The making of Waugh was the 1995 tour of the Caribbean, where he averaged 107 and stood up to the best bowler of the day, Curtly Ambrose, in a potent on-field confrontation. The drama started when Ambrose glared at Waugh after bowling a brute of a bouncer and Waugh said, 'What the fuck are you looking at? Go back and bowl.' Ambrose approached Waugh like he was going to rip him apart. Waugh met his gaze. He was perfectly still. All 5'8" of him, under the shadow of Ambrose's 6'6".

Allan Border, commentating at the time, used the power of irony to illustrate what was happening. 'They're exchanging a few words out there, batsman and bowler. Just shows you how serious those two are.' And then, 'I'm enjoying this from 150 yards away.'

Ambrose had started to edge further into Waugh's personal space, incredulous that the Australian wasn't intimidated. Just when the incident looked like it might explode into a full-scale physical confrontation, West Indies skipper Richie Richardson stepped in and dragged his fast bowler away. Ambrose then did as Waugh originally suggested and went back and bowled. The next ball struck Waugh on the shoulder. And he managed to just avoid nicking the final ball of an over commentator Tony Cozier said would be 'discussed for many years to come'.

Some saw the confrontation as theatrics, but it was more than that. It was the moment Australia stopped being the Windies' whipping boys. We'd go on to win the series 2–1 and oversee the fall of an empire. It would be the West Indies' first series loss in 15 years.

Off the field, we have Waugh to thank for helping Australian cricketers embrace India, a country that has proved personally and financially bountiful for so many. We have him to thank for the tradition of a former player handing a debutant his Baggy Green, a style of ceremony that's now commonplace in sporting codes all over the world. And as captain, we have Waugh to thank for Australian teams aggressively trying to win games instead of playing for a draw. In his 57 Tests captaining Australia, there were 41 wins, nine losses and only seven draws, helping TV audiences and crowd sizes grow exponentially.

When Hohns ended Waugh's one-day career on 11 February 2002, it was clear the clock was ticking on his time in the Test side as well. The Australian selectors wanted to start the rejuvenation process at the end of the 2002–03 Australian summer. Waugh had other ideas. It was just a matter of an ageing body living up to the expectations of an indomitable spirit.

The kid with the teeth

At Tropfest in Sydney's Domain, 100,000 people had just seen our short film, *Wilfred*, including Will Smith, Carrie-Anne Moss, Bryan Brown and Gabriel Byrne. It should have been the happiest night of my life. It started well. The film had a great reception. Jason won Best Actor and went on stage to collect his award. Then *Wilfred* won Best Comedy, so Tony went up on stage to collect his award, because the awards for the films went to the director. Then a guy in the crowd spilled a beer on me and his mate told me I was blocking his view. On stage, Tony was yukking it up with Bryan Brown, and Jason was having an intense chat with Gabriel Byrne, while I was in the mosh pit arguing with two drunks whose favourite film of the night was *Wilfred*, but who didn't recognise me from it. I looked to the stage again, and Tony and Jason now had drinks in their hands and were getting their photos taken with Will Smith.

When I got back to Melbourne, the 'Three for Free' ad was playing on high rotation. People would wait at the door of my flat to give me cakes. Sometimes notes would be left in my letterbox saying, 'I feel so sorry for you, having those big, awful teeth. I just want to be kind to you.' Or, 'You bring out so much compassion in me.'

It wasn't all love. There were people who hated the 'Free for Free' guy. And no one hated him more than the 13-year-old boy with buck teeth who was forced to leave school because of bullying directly related to the ad. The school called the ad agency to complain. The agency's panicked response was to get me to visit the buck-toothed kid and placate him before the media got wind of the situation. 'Bring the teeth,' the agency executive said. I asked her if she was sure. 'Yeah, yeah. He'll love 'em.' But I didn't think he'd love 'em because I could take my teeth out of my mouth and put them in my pocket, whereas he was stuck with his. Nevertheless, the teeth were in my pocket when the agency executive drove me to the kid's home in a run-down area in Melbourne's west. We were taken inside as parents, children and assorted pets milled about. In the corner of this dark, crowded house was a sad-looking 13-year-old boy whose teeth bore an uncanny resemblance to the teeth I wore in the ad. We were introduced. He was a sweet kid. Everyone looked at me to produce the silver bullet of wisdom that was going to make him feel better.

I asked him what had happened at school and he told me how his fellow students had started yelling 'Free for free' at him wherever he went. And that his parents had pulled him out of school and he didn't know when he'd return, if ever. I nodded. That was terrible. I looked around to see if anyone else wanted to say something. But, no, they were happy for me to do the heavy lifting. So I tried to cheer him up with a bit of self-deprecation. I told him I'd also been bullied at school, 'but it had more to do with my personality than my teeth'. He didn't laugh. I ploughed on, desperate to find common ground. 'Although,' I said, 'my teeth used to be quite bucked as well, but ...' I caught his mother's eye. She shook her head – obviously they weren't able to afford braces for him. The kid stared at me. He wanted me to finish my sentence. 'What happened?' he asked. I mumbled something about my teeth growing into my mouth and how that sometimes can happen. The kid knew a lie when he heard one. Everyone in the room was now frowning at me as if I'd blown an opportunity to make an unhappy kid feel a little better. The advertising executive started pointing to her perfectly straight white teeth to signal that I should show him the fake teeth. I looked at the kid. He was definitely sadder now than he had been when we first walked in. I asked him if he wanted to see the teeth I wore in the ad. He said, 'No.'

As we drove over the West Gate Bridge back to the city, the ad executive apologised for speeding, but said she had to go back to the office to 'unfuck' the situation. I explained that I did everything that was asked of me and that I wasn't a mental health professional. She said I could have been 'a little more upbeat and light-hearted. But it's fine. It's done. It's over now.' I couldn't work out why she wanted me to be so relentlessly positive in the face of misery. It probably would've just made him more upset. Within a week, someone involved in making the ad was able to 'unfuck' the situation by getting the kid braces – which they probably should have done in the first place. The local paper was there to record the happy event, with the smiling 13-year-old lying in the orthodontist's chair giving the thumbs-up to the camera. And nowhere in the article was there any mention of an actor trying to placate him with a set of rubber teeth.

Meanwhile, *Wilfred* had been selected to screen at the Palais Theatre on the opening night of the

St Kilda Film Festival. I knew the festival well. I'd gone to the screenings year after year, written about it, and been rejected by it. Having a film selected for opening night briefly made me feel whole. I even had a weird sense I would meet someone at that year's festival. It wasn't like I was pining for a relationship, I just had a strong feeling it was going to happen.

Before opening night, I had to spend the day being a jobbing journo, which meant interviewing Orlando Bloom, who wasn't in the mood to be interviewed. He'd just finished filming *Ned Kelly* with Heath Ledger and Joel Edgerton and told me he could feel a cold coming on. 'I'm getting sick,' he said, catching the attention of a passing waitress. 'Can I get some water, please?'

In my research, I'd learned that not only was Orlando sometimes a noncommittal interviewee, but also that we shared a birthday. I resolved to only reach for that fun fact if the interview hit a rough patch. And 35 seconds in, I found myself saying, 'Orlando, you and I share a birthday.' It would be difficult to show you a face that gave less of a fuck.

On opening night of the St Kilda Festival, the film went well, but no potential soulmate came near me. By the time I had my first beer at the closing night party, I'd forgotten all about my premonition. Then I had a conversation with a woman about cricket. I'm sure I brought it up – I was always forcing cricket into conversations where it didn't quite fit – but she said she loved the game and used to watch it with her dad. I tried to keep my heart rate at a reasonable pace as I asked her to choose a series. She chose 80–81. I then challenged her to recite the Australian batting order from that series. She started well with Dyson and Wood, then got to Chappell and Hughes. So far so good. Then Border and Walters. Wow. And by the time she got to Bruce Yardley, I knew we'd end up getting married.

Her name was Amanda and we moved in together six weeks later. We'd barely put furniture in the apartment when my phone rang.

'Adam Zwar?'

'Yes.'

'It's Sergeant Winterbottom from Cairns Police. Got a moment?'

The first four Tests

Steve Waugh needed a career resurgence to cement his spot in the Test team, but his scores on the 2002 tours of South Africa and Pakistan were mostly mediocre and it seemed selectors, the media and some of Waugh's teammates were convinced the 2002–3 Ashes series would be his last. Even Richie Benaud said he was a 'condemned man'. It was just the right amount of adversity to bring out Waugh's best.

But the fightback didn't start well. He scored 7 and 12 in the First Test in Brisbane, which Australia won by 384 runs. In the Second Test in Adelaide, which Australia won by an innings and 51 runs and where Ponting scored his second century in two Tests, Waugh managed 34. When Waugh arrived for the Third Test in Perth, Hohns visited his hotel room again to tell him that the fifth Ashes Test in Sydney 'might be a good place to finish'. Waugh told Hohns he wasn't sure. According to Waugh's book, the conversation had been low-key and amicable, but Hohns spoke to the media immediately afterwards, saying, 'At the moment, Stephen has our support until the Sydney Test.' Waugh knew that if 'Stephen has our support' wasn't the final nail in the coffin, then 'until the Sydney Test' certainly was.

The captain bounced back in Australia's win in Perth with 53, then scored 77 in the first innings in Melbourne, where he looked to have rediscovered some form. But chasing a small total in the second innings, Waugh played what he would later call his 'worst innings in Test cricket'. Just two minutes before Damien Martyn was dismissed, Waugh began to feel a migraine coming on. Then, as he walked out to bat, his head started throbbing and he worried that he was going to fall over. Waugh's first scoring shot was a heart-stopping inside edge for four. Three balls later, he nicked one off Steve Harmison through to wicketkeeper James Foster. Foster started to appeal but pulled back when he realised he was alone. Captain Nasser Hussain said the singing from the Barmy Army had drowned out any ball-on-bat noise.

When the replay on the big screen showed Waugh clearly edged the ball, Foster tried appealing in full voice, but it was too late. Harmison was already on the way back to his mark and the game had moved on. Next ball, Waugh clobbered Harmison to cover on the full and Hussain took a sharp catch ... but it was a no ball. To rub salt in England's wounds, Waugh then drove Harmison's last delivery for four.

The Australian captain went on to make a comical 14 before gloving an Andy Caddick lifter into the slips. No one was impressed with Waugh's madcap cameo in a Test that Australia would win by five wickets. The media and selectors didn't know about the migraine and even if they did, it wouldn't have changed anything. As far as they were concerned, Waugh was at the end of the road.

Going into the Fifth Test in Sydney, the equation was simple – if Waugh didn't score a century, his career was over. Every sports report on every network news bulletin led with 'this will most likely be' or, more generously, 'this could be' Steve Waugh's last Test.

The Scoutmaster

Sergeant Winterbottom explained that he was from the Cairns Police Child Protection Squad and asked me if I remembered going on a Scout camp to Fitzroy Island when I was 13. I must've sounded a little uncertain because Sergeant Winterbottom fast-tracked the conversation.

'Well, mate, you were there,' he said. 'I'm looking at a photo right now, of you and your Scoutmaster, who we're about to charge with four counts of child abuse. Some of the charges relate to incidents that happened on this trip to Fitzroy Island.'

Then it hit me. Of course I remembered the camp. I used to talk about it all the time. I remembered the last night cooking damper around a campfire and the Scoutmaster bringing his dodgy mate to the island, and his mate running a knife over my shirtless torso in an attempt to explain how you skin a person. He creepily ran the point of the knife down my chest and stomach several times – each run about 5 cm to the right of the last – showing the other Scouts that when you skin someone, you tear off the skin in individual strips. I remembered that moment vividly because I should've been scared, but my trust in adults was absolute.

Then the Scoutmaster told us we wouldn't be sleeping in our tents that night – we'd be sleeping on the beach. I remembered taking my sleeping bag onto the beach and having the best sleep of my life. That's why I remembered Fitzroy Island, in the context of sleeping on beaches. Whenever a conversation came up about sleep, I'd say with great authority that I slept well on beaches, all based on a survey of one sleep, on one beach, on one night.

Sergeant Winterbottom was grateful for my recollections and said it was 'just the type of information that'll help put this monster behind bars'. He then said he'd been trying to track me down for weeks. A trial had been set for Tuesday and they might need to fly me up to Cairns for it. 'We'll let you know.'

I said I'd be happy to help but would like to see the photo of me and the Scoutmaster on Fitzroy Island if that was OK. He explained that something was wrong with the police station's firewall and he couldn't email out, but he'd fax it to me before he knocked off.

An hour later, I watched as the fax chugged through. It showed a black-and-white image of a beach, then two adult feet with heavy boots and socks, then hairy calves, lying on the sand. They were my Scoutmaster's legs. The chugging fax then revealed a small child's feet, then calves, inside the legs of the Scoutmaster. These were my feet, my calves, naked, vulnerable, inside the Scoutmaster's legs, as both of us sat in the sand. A feeling of panic came over me. It wasn't clear what was happening. I willed the fax to spit out the whole image faster so I could work out what was going on. But then a smear of dark ink spread across the rest of the image. I pulled the fax from the machine. All that was visible were my two skinny legs inside the hairy legs of my Scoutmaster. I had no recollection of what we were doing. Was I even awake? Was it day or night? I couldn't tell. Fuck. This was terrible.

I showed the fax to Amanda, who agreed that it didn't look great and suggested I call the sergeant back straightaway to resend or at least tell us what was in the picture. I called, but all I got was a voicemail saying he'd left for the weekend and would respond to all messages on Monday morning. What kind of police station closes for the weekend, after sending a deeply alarming fax to a potential victim? I was torn between wanting time to fly so we could get to Monday morning as soon as possible, and never wanting Monday morning to arrive. What were my legs doing inside his legs?!

That weekend, I re-evaluated my life. I was needy, thin-skinned, a catastrophiser. I experienced high anxiety and low depression. Could there be a reason for my shaky mental health? I couldn't sleep on Friday, Saturday or Sunday nights, anticipating Monday and finding out the awful truth of the image.

On Monday morning, I called Cairns Police. But Sergeant Winterbottom was briefing prosecution and no one else could find the offending photograph of me and the Scoutmaster. I decided to go into the *Sunday Herald Sun* to research a story I was writing, and the new chief of staff asked me if I could interview Bryan Brown the next day. I said I couldn't. He looked at me sharply. He was a thick-necked British guy who'd previously worked at *The Sun* in London. I knew he was waiting for me to say I had an acting gig so he could tell me acting wasn't a real man's job. But when I explained I might be going to Cairns to testify against my old Scoutmaster, he softened and gently corrected my grammar. 'You mean former Scoutmaster,' he said. 'Unless he's also old, in which case you are correct.'

I explained he was facing four charges of child abuse and the chief of staff asked if I'd been molested. I said I didn't know. He was sympathetic – more sympathetic than I'd ever seen him before. Maybe he'd become more compassionate since he'd arrived in Australia. He hugged me, and said in his sweetest voice, 'It might help if you wrote about it.'

Sergeant Winterbottom called back later that afternoon and said, 'We've got the monster!' The Scoutmaster had pleaded guilty to all four counts, so I didn't have to fly to Cairns to give evidence. He then emailed through the photograph ... and it was completely innocent. It simply showed me sitting on the beach – in front of the Scoutmaster, me wide-eyed and smiling, happily playing on the beach in broad daylight.

The chief of staff later walked past my desk and a little too excitedly asked if I was going to write about being molested. I said it turned out I hadn't been. He tried to look relieved, but I could tell he was disappointed.

Amanda and I had been together for about ten months when I botched an attempt to ask her to marry me.

I didn't want to be a cliché with my proposal, and that was my first mistake. Readers, if you're thinking of proposing to someone, be a cliché. That's the way to do it – traditional. Don't try to add Tabasco, like I did. Just get on one knee, with a ring, and ask them to marry you. Don't do a treasure hunt late at night with the proposal at the end of it. And when your would-be spouse looks slightly confused, don't then lose your nerve and withdraw the proposal.

A mere six months later, I did end up asking Amanda to marry me in an extremely orthodox way and we organised a modest wedding, which leads to my second bit of advice: get a professional wedding videographer. Even if you have to take out a loan to do it. The guy I arranged to film the ceremony didn't show up, so we roped in one of our guests to do the job at the last minute. He must've been stressed because he buttoned-on when he meant to stop filming and buttoned-off when he meant to film. So what we were left with was a moody, avant-garde video of people's feet ... which is only now starting to get funny.

The last ball of the day

I watched Waugh's do-or-die innings in the Fifth Test in Sydney from the offices of the *Sunday Herald Sun*, ignoring my work and pacing up and down in front of the TV. England had made 362 in the first innings, and when Langer mistimed a hook shot and was caught in the deep, Australia found itself in trouble at 3–56.

Instead of taking his time walking out to the middle for what might've been his final Test innings, Steve Waugh 'sprinted' out there. He said he had a feeling there'd be a lot of applause and wanted to get onto the ground quickly, so he didn't 'soak up too much of that goodwill and forget about the job at hand'.

Waugh started his innings efficiently, punching the ball all over the ground and giving away no chances. When Waugh was in his 40s, Andrew Denton came out onto the ground with the drinks. That threw me, but it didn't throw the commentators enough to mention it. Turned out Denton had paid a couple of thousand dollars at a charity auction to be the assistant coach of the team for a day. And it just happened to be *that* day.

In the documentary *Perfect Day*, Denton describes serving Waugh Gatorade and the ensuing conversation. 'I said, "How you going?" And he's taking his helmet off and it's dripping with sweat. He said, "I'm enjoying myself." And he has the drink and I'm thinking, "What's the protocol here? Are you meant to say something?" So, as I left, I just said, "Don't be home before six." And wandered off.'

Waugh continued to play a chanceless innings. He was timing the ball well and his big shots kept finding gaps. But when Damien Martyn and then Martin Love were dismissed, the capacity crowd started to grow edgy. They wanted a century from Waugh and the worst-case scenario was that he would run out of batting partners. Or get run out. Gilchrist had only been in the middle for a short time before Waugh called him through for a single after hitting the ball firmly to mid-off. Waugh scampered, it was tight, and the fielder threw down the stumps at the bowler's end. The replay showed Waugh was well in, but the crowd was restless as it waited for the third umpire's decision. And it retained its nervous murmur even when it learned Waugh was not out. Everyone was on tenterhooks, and it was the same in the offices of the *Sunday Herald Sun*. Most of the staff were standing at their desks, watching one of three televisions situated around the office, arms folded, shifting weight from foot to foot. Phone calls were ignored.

At around 5.45 pm, Waugh brought up his 10,000th run in Test cricket with a slashing cut shot to the boundary. He was the third man to do it – behind Sunil Gavaskar and Border. The crowd was on its feet. Whatever was happening in the middle of the SCG, those 48,000 spectators were a big part of it.

By 6 pm Waugh was on 80 – still not enough to avoid the axe. I was dreading hearing the line from the commentary box: 'And it's goodbye to our New South Wales and Victorian viewers as they go to the news.' It would have to be a big event for them not to go to the news. I'd only known broadcasters to delay it when a match was nearing a dramatic conclusion, not when a guy was trying to reach his century.

Then Tony Greig calmed our restless hearts. 'We'll be staying with the cricket until Steve Waugh either gets his 100 or gets out,' he said. 'That's at least what we'll be doing.' That was big. The delay to the 6 pm bulletin legitimised the event as something of national significance. Most of the country knew the equation – a century means Waugh stays. Anything less, and he goes.

For the final over of the day, Waugh was on strike. He was on 95. Off spinner Richard Dawson's first two deliveries hit Waugh on the pad. The third ball he blocked.

'The entire team, and everyone related to the team, gathered on the balcony and there was just dead silence,' Denton said in *Perfect Day*.

Waugh struck the fourth ball through cover for three. It was a solid shot, but problematic because it put Gilchrist on strike with just two balls to go. Gilchrist needed a single so Waugh could face the final ball, bring up his century and get the selectors off his back. He didn't want to have to sleep on it overnight and try to get the job done the following morning.

Gilchrist said he had visions of stuffing it up and being booed off by 40,000 people. Instead, he glanced the ball past square leg for a single and the crowd cheered like he'd saved someone's life.

Then everyone got nervous all over again. One ball to go. Waugh was on 98. Hussain held up proceedings by moving the field and talking to Dawson. It was second-rate gamesmanship. The crowd booed and Waugh gave him a dirty look. Hussain would later describe the look as 'utter disdain'.

Dawson bowled, a fast ball, well pitched. Most would've defended, but Waugh's wrists were lightning fast and he drove through extra cover.

Bill Lawry: 'He's gone for it. There it is!'

The ball skidded across the SCG turf and into the boundary rope. It was skill. It was also a miracle. Waugh had scored his 29th Test century, equalling Sir Donald Bradman's record.

Bill Lawry: 'A great moment in the history of Australian Test cricket.'

Meanwhile, on ABC Radio, the silky voiced Jonathan Agnew took the emotion to another level. 'That. Is. Ext-rah-ordinary. And Steve Waugh, a man of little emotion, can barely restrain himself now. His helmet's off. Oh, he's waving his bat. Alec Stewart shakes his hand. You could not have scripted anything more remarkable than what we have seen here this afternoon.'

There was a sustained roar from the crowd as Waugh held his hands aloft. Everyone in the *Sunday Herald Sun* newsroom was in tears. And, weirdly, I received text messages from all around the country simply because I was the person my friends and family thought of when they thought of cricket.

In the dressing room after play, selectors Allan Border and David Boon congratulated Waugh.

Waugh's dad, Rodger, spoke to Prime Minister John Howard. The PM asked him how he'd coped and Rodger said he was a blubbering mess. Hundreds of fans didn't leave the ground, instead they stood outside the players' viewing area, chanting Waugh's name in an attempt to get him to come out onto the balcony. And he did. Twice. Like royalty.

'The crowd were all shouting for Steve,' Denton said. 'And I bet this is the only time in his career he's ever done this. He actually came out again and sort of waved to the crowd. And uh, you know, he's a very self-contained man, Steve, and this is one of those great moments in his career. You could just see it on him. He just had that look of "I've done it."'

I messaged Denton to ask how he felt about that day 18 years later. 'I have a framed photo of Steve and I in the dressing rooms after,' Denton wrote back. 'He signed it – "To the super coach. I couldn't have done it without you." LIFE DOES NOT GET BETTER.'

The next day, Waugh continued his heroic innings and was out the fifth ball he faced, not adding to his overnight total. It was irrelevant.

England would win the Test by 225 runs. That wasn't relevant either. Another Ashes to Australia, 4–1. Steve Waugh would go on to captain Australia for 13 more tests, winning eight of them and scoring three more centuries before retiring in Sydney in January 2004. Rahul Dravid wrote that Waugh's final innings of 80 was a typical one for the Australian captain: 'Mind over matter, a man not in form but soldiering on, taking his team to safety.' And that's how I remember him. The grit. The determination. The ability to persist when things weren't going his way. When Steve Waugh batted I felt I wasn't getting a lesson in cricket, but a lesson in life.

CHAPTER 11

2005 Ashes Tour of England

'If the French noblesse had been capable of playing cricket with their peasants, their chateaux would never have been burned.'

– GM Trevelyan, 1942

In 2005, Steve Harmison cracked Justin Langer on the elbow with his second ball in the First Test at Lord's. It was a ball that just seemed to explode off the wicket and fill English hearts with hope. England's *Cricket Monthly* wrote: 'Here was a bully being bullied. We could bloody well do this.'

Not long after, another Harmison bouncer clipped Ponting on the cheek, a wound that bled so profusely it required a trip to hospital and eight stitches. These were important moments. The aggression showed that England was different this time around. They were up for the fight.

In my time following the game, I hadn't seen a properly aggressive England attack. They'd produced killers before like Harold Larwood, Freddy Trueman and Frank Tyson, but since the early 1980s there'd been a lot of mid-level fast bowling. Bob Willis was the best of the lot and he ripped through us a couple of times, but he wasn't giving the Australians any Malcolm Marshall–style nightmares. Devon Malcolm was genuinely quick, but not a wicket-taker. Andy Caddick had his days, but he went grey in his late 20s and it sometimes looked like our guys were facing their dad. My favourite was the workhorse Angus Fraser, whose laborious approach to the wicket was famously described as being 'like a man who had his braces caught on the sightscreen'. By contrast, England's 2005 pace quartet was nasty. Harmison had a lethal short ball, Andrew Flintoff was almost unplayable as he swung the ball away from our left-handers, Simon Jones reversed it and Matthew Hoggard was pinpoint accurate.

Australia's mediocre first innings of 190 was quickly forgotten when McGrath helped skittle England for 155 in reply. We followed up with 384, leaving the home side a target of 420 to win. McGrath and Warne bundled them out for 180 and it was Groundhog Day for the all-conquering Aussies.

After play, two significant things happened. The first was that England captain Michael Vaughan sat his team down and said, 'Lads, this is gone. It doesn't get spoken about again. We're starting the series again at Edgbaston.' With the slate clean, they all went home.

Australia then did something many of its players now regret. Justin Langer, the custodian and leader of the team song, led the squad into the empty England dressing room, where Vaughan had addressed his troops only an hour or so before, and they sang 'Under the Southern Cross I Stand'. As far as acts of hubris went, this was much bolder than Slater sniffing cigars on the morning of the fourth day of the Second Test in Kolkata in 2001. This was the equivalent of giving England the middle finger. Brett Lee said he believed the incident was problematic from a karma perspective. Warne said it was cocky. Ponting, who had taken over as captain the year before, said if he'd had fewer beers, he wouldn't have done it. And Gilchrist said he sang the song with more unease than at any other time.

They were right to be wary. If you're going to upset the cricketing gods, don't do it at Lord's. That's where they all reside.

MiDa 10

Jason and I were still at the stage where we were making a lot of stuff for free. The only progression was that we'd graduated from short films and were now making TV pilots. It was a grind. We would tell each other every time someone asked us to do something for nothing that it was a 'great opportunity'. But you can't eat opportunity. We'd roped in Tony Rogers to be part of the gamble as well, and he mortgaged his house to finance a feature film script we'd written about a Russell Crowe–type celebrity living a Gatsby-style existence in country Victoria. The film was called *Rats and Cats* and its quiet dignity saw it selected for the Melbourne International Film Festival and South by Southwest film festival in Austin, Texas. It didn't make anyone any money, but it did earn me my first online trolls. According to their profile photos, my trolls were mostly white men between 30 and 45, wearing wraparound sunnies and holding up fish they'd just caught. 'The more the film went on,' one wrote, 'the more I hated Adam Zwar.'

Jason, Tony and I had one more play left in us. We pooled the prizes we'd won for *Wilfred*, which included camera hire and film stock, and turned the seven-minute short into a 22-minute TV pilot. Once we locked the edit, the producers put a dog collar around the DVD case before sending it off to every network in Australia. And every network in Australia promptly said it wasn't interested. SBS sent through the most gentle rejection, saying they liked what we'd shot but didn't think the concept would sustain a series. Then there was a break in the clouds. The Comedy Channel said it *might* be interested. That was all the encouragement Jason and I needed to set about writing eight episodes on spec in the hope that we could turn a 'might' into a 'yes'. Just as we'd finished writing the final episode, the Comedy Channel called to say it was no longer interested.

That did it for Jason and me. Our self-belief had been eroding for some time and that last bit of news made it collapse. We'd decided that trying to turn *Wilfred* into a TV show would be our last shot as a duo. Now that hadn't worked, it was time to go our separate ways. Jason's final words to me as I left his apartment were, 'I love you, mate. But I hate us.'

Returning to journalism was no longer an option. I'd been away too long and the *Sunday Herald Sun* and the *Sunday Magazine* had moved on.

What saved me from financial oblivion was voice over work. The idea to get into it started in the late 90s when a friend, who wasn't even in the entertainment industry, said he thought I could be 'one of those voice over guys'. Emboldened by the compliment, I transcribed a bunch of ads off the television and radio, hired a studio for an hour and recorded a version of how those ads would sound with my voice. I then sent the reel out to advertising agencies and sound studios and heard nothing. I wasn't deterred. Every couple of years, I'd update the reel and send it out again. There was never a response, but I kept doing it and by 2003 two creatives working on the Ford account heard my reel and gave me a chance. I was raw, but they persisted. The ads got traction and suddenly other brands started hiring me to voice their products. Soon my client list included Ford, Australia Post, iSelect, James Boag, Bundaberg Rum, Yoplait, AHM, Blackmores and of all things, the *Herald Sun*.

The voice over industry in Australia is a little secret society. If you're going to be part of it, you need to know that when you say 'Toyota', make sure you really hit the final 'T'. You can't say 'Toyoda'. Whereas it's not MiTre 10, it's MiDa 10. Know those things before you go in. The other stuff is more practical. If you're losing your voice or it's scratchy, get pineapple juice down your throat as quickly as possible. Don't be hungry when you record – the mic will pick up your rumbling belly. Make sure you're hydrated. No one wants to hear those clammy mouth noises – that's the voice over equivalent of farting. And warm your voice up. I do a couple of Shakespeare monologues before recording. Others sing or do tongue twisters. Just don't arrive cold. When reading the script, I get up on my toes as it helps create more energy. Voice over work is not normal talking, but it has to *sound* like normal talking. And to make talking sound normal through all the technology, you need to bring about three times the energy of normal talking.

Finally, voice over artists must be willing to put up with well-meaning but offensive comments from creatives and clients. On a film or TV set, it's about nurturing the actor in order to get the best performance out of them, and all suggestions are made with the utmost diplomacy. That memo has not made it to voice over land. Or if it has, it's been ignored. My worst experience was when I was hired to read a ten-minute script for a corporate video. I arrived at the studio in Melbourne, walked into the sound booth and before I had a chance to look at the script, the agency, listening down the line from Sydney, insisted the first take be recorded. So I read it cold. Stumbled a bit. But got through it.

Then I heard a female voice say to a male, 'What did you think?'

The male said, 'Fucking awful.'

And the female said, 'I know. And it was so hard to get him.'

Some opinions are more objective. Like the time I auditioned to be the voice of a massive international campaign that was worth a couple of hundred thousand dollars and would have helped us put a solid downpayment on a house. After the agency listened to scores of voices, it came down to me and a well-known actor who already had a property portfolio. But the agency and client couldn't decide which of us to go with. So our two audition tapes were played one after another to a focus group of people with electrodes stuck to their heads which measured the group's brainwaves as they heard our voices. And the other guy's voice produced marginally more enthusiastic brainwaves than mine. So he got the gig and went and bought himself a farm.

After spending a morning recording tracks for Ford dealers ('You'd be popular too, if you were selling tax-free cars and trucks'), I got a call from the producers of *Wilfred*. Unbeknownst to me, they'd rolled the dice one more time and forwarded our finished scripts to SBS. And SBS immediately got back, saying that the scripts satisfied their concerns about the concept sustaining a series and they wanted to commission it. I thought it was a prank. No Australian TV networks were commissioning experimental comedy in the mid-2000s. But SBS were serious. They even challenged us to go further with the scripts when they said, 'Turn the fucking weirdness up.' So we fucking did and *Wilfred* was slated for production in 2006.

The Second Test

After almost single-handedly winning the First Test at Lord's for Australia by taking nine wickets, McGrath went and stood on a stray cricket ball during a pre-match game of touch football at Edgbaston, tearing his lateral ligament, and was out for the match. The headline in *The Age* was 'Oooh, Aaah – there's no Glenn McGrath'. Ponting then won the toss and commentator Mark Nicholas called the Australian captain over and said, 'What are you going to do, Ricky?'

Ponting said, 'We're going to have a bowl this morning, mate.'

At that moment, you could see England captain Michael Vaughan looking into the distance, barely suppressing an excited smirk. Later Vaughan would tell Gideon Haigh that he couldn't believe his ears and had to stop himself from saying, 'You sure, mate?'

But Ponting was sure: 'With the overhead conditions the way they are. And the wicket being a couple of days behind – even after a few days of sun. Hopefully we can do some damage this morning.'

No one did any damage. The broadcast's semi-regular cutaways to McGrath, who was now watching the game from the dressing room with a pair of crutches perched beside him, tormented every Australian. England would go on to make 407, with Warne trying to fill the McGrath-sized void by chipping in with four wickets, including a ripping leg spinner to dismiss Andrew Strauss. Australia responded with 308. Then Warne collected five wickets in England's second innings as the home side capitulated for 182. Australia needed 282 to win, but none of the top six made a score over 30, leaving it up to Warne and Lee to steady the ship. And at the end of Day 3, Australia were 8 for 175, with Warne and Lee unbeaten. The equation was simple: we needed 107 runs to win with just two wickets in hand. And if we did win, we'd take an almost unassailable lead in the series.

The Age's Chloe Saltau wrote that before the final day's play, Brett Lee was getting throwdowns from Australian coach John Buchanan while Matthew Hayden, Ricky Ponting and Michael Clarke were laughing at how he couldn't seem to hit the ball.

Hearing the laughter, Lee grumbled to himself, 'It should be you guys getting the runs. You've put me in this situation.' Lee then started trying to hit Hayden, Ponting and Clarke with slogging drives ... and unexpectedly got his eye in.

In the first session Lee and Warne put on 55 runs before Warne was dismissed by treading on his stumps. We still had 62 to get and only one wicket in hand. Lee and Michael Kasprowicz then batted for an hour, boosting each other up between overs and reminding each other to 'Watch the ball like a hawk'. It worked. England's bowlers panicked. Each ball was either a bouncer or a yorker. With just four runs to bring about an unlikely win, Lee played a controlled cut shot to deep point and the Australians in the dressing room leaped out of their seats thinking they'd won ... but instead of the ball going to the boundary, it went straight to the fielder. One metre either side and we'd have been up 2–nil and nobody would've talked about Ponting's decision to bowl first. Then, with three runs to get, Kasprowicz received a short ball from Harmison, which caught his glove, went through to keeper Geraint Jones, and the umpire gave him out. Replays showed that Kasprowicz's glove wasn't on his bat at the precise moment it made contact with the ball and the laws of cricket clearly state that the glove is only considered part of the bat when it's touching the bat.

I know deep down that superstition isn't real, but the situation here was calamitous – McGrath stepping on a ball, Ponting choosing to field first, Warne treading on his stumps and a shoddy umpiring decision to seal the deal. Why did we sing the song in the England dressing room? Why was that necessary?

Next morning, the photograph of Flintoff leaning down to console a stunned Lee, sitting disconsolately on the pitch, was all over the internet as well as the front of every newspaper. What did Flintoff actually say to Lee? At after-dinner speeches, Flintoff reckons he said, 'It's 1–1, son.' But the look in Flintoff's eyes betrayed more empathy than that.

Lee later confirmed that he said, 'You cheeky little bugger, you almost got us.'

Wilfred – the TV series

The issue on *Wilfred* was my hairline. It had been four years since we shot the short film and two years since we shot the pilot, and because we were using footage from both to make the series, we had to match what my hairline looked like in those heady days. The hair and make-up team suggested a wig, but Tony said 'no wigs'. In fact, he was quite emotional about it: 'There'll be no wigs!' The hair and make-up team said the wig wouldn't *look* like a wig and explained the process of making it look realistic.

'NO WIGS!'

Instead of a wig, the make-up department used Hair-In-A-Can, which meant I would have to get to set an hour before everyone else so a litre of highly flammable butane, propane, iron oxides, talc and fumed silica could be sprayed onto my head. Hair-In-A-Can is a bonding agent that's meant to make your hair look more plentiful. It didn't make my hair look more plentiful. It turned it into a see-through cloud of brown and red carcinogens. But the make-up department's *pièce de résistance* was the two triangles of mesh with red hair woven into them that were glued to each of my temples. Sadly, the triangles didn't look like hair – they looked like two possums sheltering from a storm. Toward the end of filming, my left triangle went missing. It was a catastrophe. I couldn't go on camera with just one triangle and the show's budget hadn't allowed for an emergency triangle. So the crew broke into groups of twos and threes to search for the missing triangle because every minute it was at large, the production was losing thousands of dollars. No one could find it. It wasn't in the wardrobe bus, the catering tent, nor in Wilfred and Sarah's house. The search continued for more than 20 minutes, through boxes of camera and sound equipment as well as the hero car, before a loud scream was heard in Wilfred and Sarah's backyard. I recognised the emotion behind the scream – it was unique to setting eyes on a triangle and was something I'd do silently in the make-up bus every morning. By the time I walked into the backyard, the crew had formed a circle around the offending article as it hung off a branch, shivering in the breeze. It was no bigger than a wine coaster, yet it represented my vanity, my age and my vulnerability.

As the crew stared at it, I felt they were actually staring into my soul. The make-up woman asked them to give her some space as she put on latex gloves and used tweezers to remove it from the branch and deftly reattach it to the side of my head. As we made our way to the next location I apologised to the actor Kim Gyngell, who played Wilfred's vet, for all the excitement. He laughed and said, 'I fucken luvvved it!'

The Third and Fourth Tests

It was one–all going into Old Trafford, with England in the ascendancy.

Australia was rattled. McGrath was back for the Test, but failed to make an immediate impact as England won the toss and coasted to 444, with skipper Vaughan top scoring with 166. Warne and Lee chipped in with four wickets each. Warne was bowling the best he'd bowled since the mid-90s and batting better than ever. His 90-run contribution made Australia's first innings total of 302 look half decent.

In England's second dig, McGrath found some form again with five wickets and England declared at 6 for 280, leaving Australia an improbable 423 to get in a day and a bit. Wickets fell at regular intervals, with Flintoff bagging four. Ponting's 156 was a captain's knock in the spirit of Waugh and Border. When he gloved one down the leg side, Australia were suddenly 9 for 354, leaving Lee and McGrath to see out the final 24 balls. England fancied their chances, but Lee was a strong batter and McGrath had been receiving intensive batting lessons from Steve Waugh and had come a long way since Richie Benaud famously said, 'Glenn McGrath dismissed for two, just 98 runs short of his century'. When the two quicks held on for a tense draw, the jubilant Australian squad spilled onto the playing area after the final ball to congratulate them. It was the decent thing to do, but that triggered something in Vaughan. He suddenly saw this all-conquering team celebrating a draw as if it were a victory. That meant they were vulnerable. Australia was hanging on for dear life.

The form of everyone, apart from Warne, had been sporadic. And now, on the eve of the Fourth Test, McGrath was injured again. It wasn't his ankle this time, but an old elbow injury that had flared up.

I am the ultimate optimist when it comes to Australian cricket. I will the team to victory even when victory isn't an option. I'm delusional enough to think my enthusiasm will actually have an effect, but with McGrath gone and England coming home with a wet sail, I couldn't see a path to victory. The selectors had lost faith in Jason Gillespie, who had taken three wickets at 100 for the series, and replaced him for the Fourth Test with 22-year-old tearaway Shaun Tait. So our pace attack consisted of Lee, who had only just returned to Test cricket after spending 18 months on the outer; Kasprowicz, who had been dropped for the Third Test to make way for McGrath; and debutant Tait. I wondered if selectors thought of bringing in Stuart MacGill on that turning Trent Bridge deck – two wrist spinners could have been lethal – but it didn't happen. Things went from worse to worst after Vaughan won the toss. England batted first and made 477. Australia responded with 218; Lee top scoring with 47.

Then, shame of all shames, we were made to follow-on. The last time Australia had followed-on was Karachi in 1988. Graeme Wood was still in the team. 'Simply Irresistible' was number one. We batted better in the second innings and were 2 for 155 when Ponting was run-out by substitute fielder Gary Pratt, whose direct hit changed the course of the match and potentially the series. Ponting had already complained about England not using a traditional 12th man in the series. Instead, whenever an England bowler left the field between spells, he'd be replaced by a Jonty Rhodes–style super-fielder plucked from County cricket. Pratt was the best of the lot. So Ponting was already in a state of high anxiety when he made his way back to the dressing room and caught England coach Duncan Fletcher smiling cheekily at him from the balcony. Fletcher would later claim he was smiling because he burned the toast he was making. But Ponting read his smile as a gloat – the self-satisfied grin of a man whose devious tactics had worked – so he gave him an earful. This incident would eventually change the rules of the game regarding bowlers leaving the field and who could replace them. But at that moment, Fletcher kept on grinning. He knew it was the play that had won England the Ashes. Australia would go on to make 387 in the second innings, leaving England 129 to win. The home side got the runs with three wickets in hand. Warne picked up four in that innings and eight for the match. But to what end? England were now 2–1 up. Australia could still tie the series with a win at The Oval, which would mean we'd retain the Ashes, but the victory would be hollow. You couldn't say England was the better team. But they were definitely the more organised team and luck was on their side.

Bodyline

A documentary producer sat in my agent's office and told us he was looking for someone to host a documentary for the ABC about the 1932–33 Bodyline series. He quickly followed up by saying he didn't want me to get my hopes up as he'd be casting the net wide to find the right host. I nodded. He then asked if I knew anything about Bodyline.

It was surprising to see a documentary being made on a topic that I actually knew something about. And although I really wanted to give him the TED-Talk version beginning with Bodyline's leg theory origins which dated back to the early 1900s, I'd recently learned that people don't need to know everything that's going on in your head. So I kept it brief and told him that 'Bodyline' was developed by England captain Douglas Jardine for the 1932–33 Ashes series and involved putting most of his team's fielders on the leg side then bowling fast and short at the batter's body. I explained that when facing this kind of delivery, the batter had two choices: he could either allow himself to be hit or put his bat in between the ball and his body to protect himself. In doing the latter, he wouldn't have much control over the ball and was likely to pop up a simple catch to the packed leg side field. I neatly finished my soliloquy by saying that Jardine had developed the tactic to neutralise Bradman, who'd averaged 139 in the previous Ashes.

The producer nodded casually, as if all the other potential hosts he'd spoken to had answered the question with the same detail. I was curious to hear what Richard Wilkins had said.

Producer: 'Who was Jardine's greatest weapon?'

AZ: 'Harold Larwood. He was fast and accurate enough to bowl the narrow, neck-high channel that Bodyline demanded.'

Producer: 'What did the Australian Board of Control say in its cable to the MCC?'

AZ: 'That it was "unsportsmanlike".'

Producer: 'What was the MCC's response?'

AZ: 'They wanted us to retract the word "unsportsmanlike" and we did. And it wasn't until the West Indies bowled Bodyline against England in 1933 that the MCC changed the rules so it could never happen again.'

The producer offered me the gig. I accepted. Then he told me his plan was to illustrate what Bradman was up against, by getting the host to face a Test fast bowler without a helmet and was that something I was willing to do? It would be insane of me to put myself in that kind of jeopardy. I was just starting to make some progress with my career, I wasn't ready to be hit in the head and immobilised for life.

So I said: 'Sure. As long as the person bowling at me isn't Brett Lee.' At that stage, Lee had sent down the second-fastest delivery ever at 161.1 km/h, just behind Pakistan's Shoaib Akhtar, who'd been clocked at 161.3 km/h.

The producer laughed a 'don't be ridiculous' kind of laugh at the Lee suggestion. And I laughed like someone who'd just said something ridiculous. And my agent laughed at how quickly deals come together when you have a client willing to face express pace without a helmet.

The documentary would take a long time to make. The first sequence we filmed was straight out of the *MythBusters* playbook, where a visual effects artist used footage of an over from the 1933 Adelaide Test to construct a 3D video of Larwood bowling. The video was sent to the Australian Institute of Sport, where they were able to track Larwood's speed as being 147 km/h. Not bad for a bowler who was only 5'7". But Larwood had a textbook run-up that built slowly in velocity as he approached the crease before he used his massive upper-body strength and disproportionately long arms to hurl down a 147 km/h missile. Bear in mind, his bowling speed was measured at 147 km only in the over that was transferred to 3D. It's unlikely that this was his fastest over on the Ashes tour.

The producer weighed up the pros and cons of me facing the Test fast bowler, who still hadn't been locked in. If we didn't go through with it, we wouldn't have an ending. If we did, I might die. I didn't tell Amanda or Dad the gory details of what we were planning because I didn't want to alarm them. And there'd be plenty of time for them to learn all about it when they read eyewitness accounts of the disaster in the paper afterwards. Meanwhile, the hand-wringing from all of us inside the production made the film less a historical documentary and more a story about a freaked-out actor preparing to put his life on the line. The foolhardy nature of the exercise was thrown into relief the day we interviewed a brain surgeon, who explained what would happen if I were hit in the head with a cricket ball travelling in the high 140s. He calmly said it would cause acute arterial bleeding, and although I would probably be alert immediately after impact, I would soon slip into deep unconsciousness as the clot of blood became progressively bigger and squashed my brain. And then I would die.

'That's why we have helmets,' he said. I looked at the producer. The producer looked away.

After that conversation, the producer decided he needed to know if I had the ability to avoid getting hit in the head, so I was taken to the Victorian Institute of Sport, fitted with a laser eye tracker, and told to stand in front of a video projection of a bowler running in to bowl. The eye tracker recorded where my eyes were looking at the point of delivery. An elite batter looks at the bowler's grip, the bowler's arm movement and the release of the ball – whereas I looked at the bowler's face. The guy operating the software said my eye movements were common among 'unskilled players' but my reflexes were quick enough to get out of the way once I'd focused on the ball.

Our concerns were allayed by the comment about my reflexes right up until the moment I interviewed Matthew Hayden. We were coming to the end of a discussion about Bradman when I asked if he had any advice for a helmetless batter facing someone bowling in the high 140s.

Matthew Hayden: 'Is that what you're going to do?'

AZ: 'Yeah, it's going to be the climax of the film.'

MH: 'Don't do it.'

AZ: 'Would you do it?'

MH: 'Mate, I've released enough blood in my time. Had my teeth knocked out. I've broken hands. Am I making you feel better about this? There's no chance I'd do it.'

AZ: 'Any advice?'

MH: 'Eyes to the barrel. You've got to watch the ball. That's my only advice.'

AZ: 'That's the problem. I've just done a laser tracker experiment where they tracked my eyes at the point of delivery, and they found I watched the bowler's face and not the ball.'

Hayden grinned.

MH: 'You're an actor, mate. You don't need to prove anything to anyone. You don't have to be Bradman. Just get out of the way of it. If it bowls you, it bowls you. Just avoid it at all costs, I reckon. I mean, hopefully it's not someone too Larwood-like. Not Brett Lee or anyone like that.'

The whole set went quiet. Haydos looked around at the producer.

MH: 'Seriously, it's not Brett Lee, is it?'

The Fifth Test

There wasn't much pride to salvage in the Fifth Test at The Oval. But if we won, we'd at least retain the

Ashes and extend our 16-year stretch of holding on to them. The whole series had been a rude shock for Australian cricket fans, who weren't comforted by the hollow aphorisms of sportswriters who had said it had been 'good for cricket'.

Michael Vaughan won the toss for the third time in a row. The last time Ponting won it was when he elected to bowl in Edgbaston, so the cricketing gods had clearly decided he could not be trusted with a correct call.

Like the rest of the series, the game was tight, but England had its nose in front. Batting first, the home side made 373 thanks to a century from Strauss. Australia's response started strongly. Langer and Hayden's opening stand was 185, with both openers scoring centuries. Hayden, whose form in the series had been disappointing, saved himself from career oblivion by taking a careful approach to his innings. Then Ponting put up a bit of a fight before Flintoff rolled us for 363. Gilchrist's score of 23 meant he didn't score a 50 in the series. He would later write that the 2005 Ashes was the worst time in his cricketing life. Flintoff unpicked him by going around the wicket in what was more happy accident than grand masterplan. The England all-rounder was forced to go around the wicket to the Aussie keeper in a pre-Ashes one-dayer because the over-the-wicket footmarks were too deep. And he got him. So he thought he'd try it again. And he got him again. He would end up dismissing him four times in five Tests.

In England's second innings, Australia was still in with a chance when we had them 7–199. But Kevin Pietersen's maiden Test century meant England cruised to 335, nullifying any hope of Ashes retainment. The Barmy Army were onto it and started chanting, 'You're only good at swimming', which is patently unfair: we're also good at sailing.

That left Australia a target of 341 in 19 overs, and only four balls were bowled before bad light put us out of our misery. I immediately turned the TV off for fear of seeing happy English faces.

The series was a masterclass in humbling a champion team. Players who had dominated for so long were forced to take stock. Ponting's captaincy was criticised for being unimaginative and the batting averages were ordinary – Hayden 35, Langer 43, Ponting 39, Clarke 37, Martyn 19, Katich 27 and Gilchrist 22. We didn't make 400 once. And on the bowling side, it was all about McGrath and Warne. McGrath took 19 wickets in three Tests at 23 while Warne took 40 wickets in five Tests at 19. Meanwhile, Lee was the best of the rest of the bowlers, taking 20 wickets at 41, followed by Tait who took five wickets at 42, Kasprowicz who took four wickets at 62, and Gillespie three wickets at 100. The moral of all these stats was that Warne and McGrath covered a lot of cracks. And in the three Tests that McGrath played, he was only fully fit in one of them.

The *Daily Telegraph* led the hand-wringing back home with the headline 'THE END', but it was unclear if it was referring to the series, certain careers, Australian cricket or the world. *The Age* was less cryptic when it thundered that 'Today, Australians know how it felt to be English'.

The Poms caught an arrogant bear napping. Vaughan and Fletcher were well prepared and Flintoff was heroic. Everything went right for them. The big test would be how they handled being given MBEs and paraded through the streets like war heroes.

CHAPTER 12

2006–7 Ashes in Australia

'I tend to believe that cricket is the greatest thing God ever created on Earth.'

– Harold Pinter

The first season of *Wilfred* had been delivered to SBS and, as the on-air date approached, our first review appeared on my Google alerts. I made myself a cup of tea and excitedly sat down to read it. Here are some extracts:

'The "joke" wears off in about four seconds.'

'... discerning viewers will be left wondering who on earth commissioned this idea.'

'It would be unoriginal and churlish of us to call this a "dog" of a show ... but it is.'

'Give it a very wide berth for the next eight weeks.'

I got light-headed after reading that. It's a strange phenomenon to pour your heart and soul into something for the equivalent of $2 an hour over many years and then be publicly shamed for it. We had put so much energy into this – the fighting over scripts, the fighting over casting, the fighting over the edit. Maybe the critic would have been more sympathetic if he'd seen us fighting over the dog suit.

I tried lifting myself off the canvas. Everyone would read this, so my career in entertainment was over. And no one was really hiring journalists anymore. I'd started becoming quite proficient at making crepes – so I toyed with the idea of opening a food truck.

My cycle of catastrophising was broken when James Hewison, head of the Australian Film Institute and champion of our feature film *Rats and Cats*, asked if I'd be interested in writing Geoffrey Rush's script for that year's AFI Awards. A time was arranged to go around to Geoffrey's house. I turned up a little too early and rang the doorbell. His wife, Jane, answered. 'Don't be scared,' she said, clocking the panic in my eyes.

It was weird. I didn't get scared interviewing celebrities. I knew that job. But this was different. What if I couldn't think of anything funny to write? Or, worse, what if I could, and the Oscar-BAFTA-Tony-Emmy winner didn't like it? A reviewer not liking my jokes made me wobbly on my feet. Geoffrey not liking them would probably finish me off.

There was no need to worry. L'Oréal Paris sponsored the awards that year and Geoffrey wrote the first joke: 'I'm the face of L'Oréal Paris that went horribly, horribly wrong.' After that, we were off to the races.

I wrote a sketch called 'AFI Anonymous' where past AFI Award winners met every Tuesday to discuss how they had been unable to get a job since winning their award. And I cut together a bunch of Demtel–style ads spruiking a fake DVD box set featuring all of Geoffrey Rush's better, earlier work such as Detective Number #1 in *Hoodwink*, the Floor Manager in *Starstruck* and Peter the Priest in *Menotti*. 'And if you call in the next 25 seconds, we'll throw in *On Our Selection* absolutely free.' Both sketches would go on to kill in the room thanks to the inside jokes and free wine. But if you were watching from home and feeling generous, you might've found them moderately amusing.

Geoffrey was fine about me having the cricket on in the living room while we worked. I don't think he cared much for sport, but he recognised obsession. There was one thing that slowed down our work process – every time he wanted to google something, he would save and close the Word document we were working on, boot up Firefox, google the information, then close Firefox, before opening the Word file again. After watching him do this for days, I summoned the courage to show him that opening a search engine didn't affect the status of a Word document. He seemed grateful.

It became clear that the reason Geoffrey was so successful wasn't just about talent – it was because he put in more hours than anyone else. He didn't chitchat or idle. He toiled over jokes and characters and constantly wrestled with the tone of the show. Sometimes I'd have to remind him that we needed to eat, and we'd go down the road and get pies for lunch. He didn't drive, so when we had to meet with the AFI or record a sketch for the show, I'd take us to the venue in my 1992 Ford Telstar. The multimillionaire didn't care what car he was being driven in – it was all about the work.

One afternoon, Jane came into the office and announced that the dog had killed a possum in the backyard and could Geoffrey please bury it.

'Certainly,' said Geoffrey and we headed into the yard. Geoffrey went under the house and emerged seconds later with a pristine shovel that had never been used. It was shiny and the sticker was still on it.

Geoffrey stood next to the dead possum, the sparkling shovel leaning against his hip as he rolled a cigarette and continued workshopping jokes for the show. After finishing that cigarette, he started rolling another while the shovel and possum remained in situ.

Finally, I asked, 'Geoffrey, shall I bury the possum?'

'If you would.'

Damien Martyn

It'd been 14 months since England had surgically ripped the Ashes from our overconfident hands. During that time, this mighty Australian side licked its wounds and seethed. As the First Test in Brisbane approached, we didn't come across as overconfident or cocky. Instead we looked like we were ready for a fight. On the first morning, Ponting won the toss and batted. So far, so good. The tension in the media and around the ground was palpable. Steve Harmison, one of the heroes of 2005, stormed in from the top of his mark and kicked off the 2006–07 Ashes with a delivery so wide that Flintoff caught it at second slip. Some pundits wrote that it was the moment Australia won the series. Maybe they were right – we triumphed in the First Test by 277 runs, with Ponting scoring 196.

When the Second Test in Adelaide started, it felt like England had found the groove that won them the 2005 Ashes and MBEs from the Queen. The visitors made 551 in the first innings. Australia responded with 513 thanks to centuries from Ponting and Clarke. Warne then picked up four to help dismiss England for 129 in its second innings and Australia chased down the 168 runs to win with six wickets in hand. Two–nil. Minutes after the Aussies settled into their post-match festivities, there was a knock on the door. It was England wanting to party. Beers flowed. And, as the story goes, it wasn't long before an argument broke out between Matthew Hayden and Damien Martyn. And not long after that, Martyn was suggesting Jimmy Anderson pick up a pad and whack Michael Clarke over the head with it.

At 11.15 am the next day an email without a subject line lobbed into Cricket Australia boss James

Sutherland's inbox, which soon found its way into News Limited and Fairfax newspapers. It read:

Dear James,

I would like to advise of my retirement from cricket, effective from today. I have enjoyed everything the game has given me. I have gained from it more than I could have ever imagined. I have made, in the playing of cricket, lifelong friends.

It was from Damien Martyn, who had so far scored 29, 11 and 5 in the series. He hadn't told Ponting of his decision, nor any of his teammates. And after he pressed send on the email, he went underground.

Later, in an interview with News Corp, Martyn discussed what went on with Hayden after the Adelaide Test and whether it had any influence on his decision to retire.

'We were arguing about something silly. I didn't retire because of that night. I never made the decision drinking that night. I made it before the Test even started.'

If that were the case, then why didn't Martyn alert his captain and biggest supporter, Ricky Ponting, of the decision? 'I knew if I spoke to people, I wouldn't be allowed to retire. I knew if I told Mike Hussey and Ricky, they would have tried to stop me.'

Still, Martyn was a mysterious figure in Australian cricket. He played the ball late and with superhuman ease, making batting appear so simple that it didn't look like he was trying. His international career was seven Tests old when it came undone during a tense run chase against South Africa in 1994. Australia were eight wickets down with six runs to win when the precocious 22-year-old was caught playing what looked to be a lazy cover drive on the rise. The shot exposed McGrath to a feisty South African attack and Australia lost by 5 runs. Selectors, media and fans were ropeable with what appeared to be Martyn's lack of discipline and he was banished from the Australian set-up for nearly six years.

When he came back in 2000, the cockiness was gone. He kept his head right down and averaged over 50. In 2005 he was awarded Test Player of the Year at the Allan Border Medal, but was dropped a few months later after an unproductive Ashes series. Ponting still believed in him, and the captain successfully made the case to selectors that Martyn should be taken on the 2006 tour of South Africa because he was likely to have 'an influence' when it mattered. It was a difficult decision, as taking Martyn meant leaving behind Brad Hodge, who'd scored a double century just three Tests earlier. Martyn repaid his captain's faith by scoring a match-winning century in the Third Test in Johannesburg. That was the moment when Martyn wanted to retire, but he was talked out of it by teammates.

On the morning of Martyn's email to Sutherland, Ponting was playing golf. In his *Captain's Diary*, he explained that he checked his phone after nine holes and saw a missed called from Cricket Australia's general manager, Michael Brown. When the captain returned Brown's call, he was shocked but not surprised to hear of Martyn's retirement. If he had a problem, it was the way Martyn handled his exit. 'No formal farewell to the team, no press conference, no call to me, his mate, to explain why,' wrote Ponting. 'I was frustrated because I was left answering questions about something I knew nothing about, when one media appearance by him would have cleared the air.'

If you've forgotten Marto, as I fear some have, Twitter archivist @robelinda2 has posted several feature films worth of footage from cricket's past and the clips of Martyn stand out. There, for posterity, are his imperious reverse sweeps, the ridiculous blocks for four, the graceful cutting, driving and pulling accompanied by Tony Greig saying time and again, 'Oh that's lovely. That's a lovely shot.'

Even Mark Waugh knows he has a battle on his hands for the mantle of Australia's most elegant batter. During a BBL match, Damien Fleming needled his commentary partner, Waugh, by saying, 'Junior, if I had to pick my favourite Australian batsman in my era, it would be Damien Martyn hitting through the off side and you hitting through the leg side.'

There was silence in the commentary box as the next ball was bowled. Then Waugh piped up, 'Hey Flem, I think you'll find I was pretty strong through the off side as well.'

Bodyline part 2

My love of Bodyline started when I was 11 and in bed with chickenpox. That's when my next-door neighbours, who had once banned me from playing cricket with their son because I wasn't Catholic, came through with an incredible kindness. They lent me their Betamax VCR plus all seven episodes of the Kennedy Miller–produced series *Bodyline*. During that week, I watched the series in its entirety six times. I'd walk around the house, talking in my poshest voice, pretending I was England captain Douglas Jardine, played by Hugo Weaving: 'I'm not here to win friends, I'm here to win the Eshes.'

Jardine on the ship entering Australia: 'Gentlemen, we are entering the land of the barbarian.'

And Jardine to Australian captain Bill Woodfull: 'I've come to demand an apology.'

Woodfull: 'What for?'

Jardine: 'I don't appreciate being called a bastard.'

Woodfull (addressing the Australian dressing room): 'Which one of you bastards called this bastard a bastard?'

I became obsessed with Woodfull after watching the *Bodyline* miniseries. The dour schoolteacher wasn't a Jardine–style tactician, but he was a leader of men. If you had potential, Woodfull would help you reach it. His refusal to retaliate against Jardine's Bodyline tactics pointed to his moral fortitude. Not everyone agreed with him. Minutes before the coin toss in the

Second Test in Melbourne, members of the Australian Cricket Board of Control were arguing about whether Woodfull should remain captain. Australia had lost the First Test, crumbling under Jardine's tactics, and the board was torn as to whether to stick to the high road or go with vice-captain Victor Richardson's desire to bowl Bodyline right back at England.

The board stuck with Woodfull and Australia won the Second Test. It was in the Third Test in Adelaide that Woodfull was struck on the heart by Larwood. Some say Bodyline had nothing to do with the incident as Jardine hadn't set a leg-theory-style field for that delivery, but the England captain would often flit between leg-theory fields and orthodox to create chaos in the mind of the batter as Larwood sent down short, 147 km/h grenades. After being struck, Woodfull bent down, trying to get his pain and breath under control while 52,000 fans at Adelaide Oval were shouting like they were in the Colosseum. Archive footage shows them shoulder to shoulder and heaving like a virus trying to break out of a cell wall. If just one had leapt the fence, the rest would have followed, and police wouldn't have had a hope of stopping them. The result would've been dead Englishmen and probably a dead Woodfull and Bradman, who was at the non-striker's end. Jardine hung back as his teammates went to Woodfull's aid. The England captain's only words of encouragement were reserved for Larwood. 'Well bowled, Harold,' he said pointedly as Woodfull slowly rose to his feet. Jardine then clapped his hands twice and ordered a leg-theory field. Woodfull wore many more body blows before being dismissed for 22 in 89 minutes.

Later in that same innings, when Australian keeper and World War I hero Bert Oldfield had his skull fractured from a rising Larwood delivery, Woodfull strode onto the field to take care of him. Images from the day show Woodfull, in a three-piece suit, standing by Oldfield, who's lying on the turf, blood spurting from his head. At that moment, I'm sure Woodfull would've loved to have taken revenge, but the man they called 'Old Steadfast' held his fire. He simply picked up Oldfield's bat and escorted him off the ground. Later in the match, England manager Plum Warner approached Woodfull to express his disappointment in Jardine, but the Australian captain said he didn't want to see him. 'There are two teams out there,' he famously told Warner, 'and only one of them is playing cricket.'

When Woodfull died at 67, his wife, Gwen, said the multiple chest blows Woodfull received in the Bodyline series had hastened his death.

For the Bodyline documentary, I visited Melbourne High School where Woodfull taught maths. The school's historian, Dr Alan Gregory, told the story of Woodfull returning to the school after he'd made a rare duck in a Test match and the students had teasingly written a big '0' on the board. Woodfull entered the room and, without missing a beat, drew two lines through the '0' and said, 'Prove that the two angles are equal.'

By now, we'd finished filming the history side of the Bodyline documentary and all that was left was for me to face a Test fast bowler without a helmet. The producer was keen that I not get killed while doing this, so he hired all-rounder John Hastings, who'd played for Australia in all three formats of the game, to teach me how to face express pace. John was a great coach. As the bowling machine spat out cricket balls at 145 km/h, John was patient with me in the same way that a kindergarten teacher might be patient with a kid who had learning difficulties. I knew what that looked like because I'd been one of those kids. Four decades later, nothing had changed. For instance, when teaching the pull shot, John would tell me not to thrash at the ball, but to ride with it. The footage of our conversation shows I'm listening intently to everything he's saying and nodding earnestly, then, when facing the very next ball, I thrash at it like I'm in a pillow fight.

Later, while shadow-batting in the nets and trying to lock in what I'd been taught, I saw the producer and director over by the Coke machine asking John a series of intense questions. I couldn't hear what they were saying, but the conversation didn't look like a happy one. There was a lot of shaking of heads, pitying glances over at me, then grim nods of agreement. Eventually, the producer broke from the circle and said, 'Adam, mate. When it comes time to face the fast bowler, we're thinking that instead of you actively trying to hit the ball, that it might be better if you just got out of the way.'

It was humiliating. But I'd had decades to process my lack of cricket ability and believed there was merit in not getting killed in front of the crew.

So Neil Buszard, the head coach of cricket at the Victorian Institute of Sport, was brought in to teach me how to get out of the way. He stood halfway up the wicket with a baseball glove in his hand and explained that he was going to throw a ball at my face and it was up to me to duck out of the way while never taking my eyes off it.

Sometimes I could do it. Other times I'd get hit. After these sessions, no one in their right mind would say I was ready to face an elite fast bowler, but at least now I was able to execute the plan Matthew Hayden had recommended so many months before, which was to avoid the ball at all costs.

McGrath and Warne

The Third Test in Perth was evenly poised until Hussey, Clarke and Gilchrist all scored centuries in Australia's second innings. Gilchrist's came in 57 balls, one ball slower than Viv Richards' 100 against England in 1986. Warne took four wickets to wrap up England's second innings and Australia won by 206 runs. Three–nil. The Ashes were back. Then Warne and McGrath announced that Sydney would be their final Test.

We all knew it was coming. Cricket Australia had carefully leaked the story as a rumour a few weeks earlier so the shock wouldn't be too much for our fragile hearts. If it weren't for Warne and McGrath, this world-beating Australian side which had dominated cricket for more than a decade would have been dragged right back to the peloton. Warne was the greatest spinner ever and it's hard to know which fast bowler you would pick before McGrath. Marshall? Akram? Hadlee? If you chose McGrath before any of them, no one would blame you. The fact that Warne and McGrath appeared on the national stage at the same time and played 104 Tests together was nothing short of a freak of nature. Out of those 104, they won 71 and lost just 16, accumulating 1011 wickets. The next best bowling duo was Courtney Walsh and Curtly Ambrose, who played 95 tests for 762 wickets, followed by Pakistan greats Wasim Akram and Waqar Younis, who played 61 Tests for 550 wickets.

Gideon Haigh compared Warne and McGrath to a comedy duo. 'To call them a combination, implying planning and foresight, is not quite right,' he wrote. 'They were more, as Palmerston described his coalition with Disraeli, an "accidental and fortuitous concurrence of atoms".'

It's hard to know why McGrath was so good. He wasn't that fast. And if it came down to height and bounce, why weren't Stuart Clark or Josh Hazlewood as successful? McGrath himself puts it down to psychology, saying 'natural ability' only accounts for 10 to 20 per cent of your success as a cricketer and the rest is 'mental strength'. To get a handle on that, we really need to define the parameters of 'natural ability'. I know a lot of mentally strong grade cricketers who never got a call from Trevor Hohns. I guess the difference was that every time McGrath landed the ball just short of a length and outside off stump, there was just enough bounce and variation to deceive the batter. Haigh compared McGrath to the Model T Ford, in the way that he mass-produced one exceptionally accurate delivery after another. But it's not known whether his superhuman ability to land a ball on the same awkward spot every time was honed in the dirt pitch in the backyard of his parents' poultry farm with an upturned water trough for a wicket or via former Australian coach Geoff Marsh getting him to bowl for hours at a single wicket. Probably neither. He was just a force of nature.

What I found most impressive about McGrath was how he went from looking a little bit like what well-meaning parents in the 1980s called 'special' to objectively handsome. No doubt you can thank his first wife, Jane McGrath, for that. She was cool. And smart. And we saw how much he loved her and that made us love him. And when she was hit with breast cancer at a tragically young age, our hearts broke for them both.

Then there was Warne. It wasn't just his prodigious skill and ability to take wickets – it was the theatre. His 'oooh' after every ball. Didn't matter if the batter got tangled up or hit him for six – it was always 'oooh'. It was the body language of a magician confident in his tricks.

Warne was famous for saying that 'part of the art of bowling spin is to make the batsman think something special is happening when it isn't'. But there was always stuff happening with Warne. This was a man who would plan the six balls he would bowl in any over, where each would land and what kind of stroke the batter would play. His run-up was five walked paces then three trotted paces before unleashing a ripping leg break, flipper, slider, zooter or woofer. Have I missed any? When he first started out, he spun the ball sideways. His most famous delivery of all – the 'Ball of the Century' to get Mike Gatting – turned leg spin bowling from a dead art to the thing every kid wanted to do. The headline in the Daily Express was 'WHAT A SHANE – England Rocked by Spin Wizard'. It wasn't a fluke. He constantly left genius Test batters questioning the laws of physics.

Then came the shoulder injury and surgery in 1998 that doctors told him would end his cricketing career.

But he returned, albeit gingerly. At first, he wasn't getting the purchase on the ball he once did. But it was a miracle he was out there at all. 'Biomechanically speaking, the guy is a freak,' said his leg spinning second-in-command, Stuart MacGill. 'I mean, this was a career-ending injury that didn't end his career. He just had the ability to continue on and to shape his game as his physical abilities changed.'

There was a period immediately after shoulder surgery when Warne relied mostly on theatrics and reputation to bamboozle batters and umpires. But after the '99 World Cup, he was back to a version of his old self. He may not have spun the ball as sharply, but there was more variation and bounce from one ball to the next. A delivery might land on the same spot as the previous, but arrive there from a different arc. He'd experiment with speed and bowl close to the stumps or wide of the crease. He'd always be teasing and questioning and making a big deal about moving fielders a foot to the left or right. His masterstroke, though, was the incredulous look he'd give an umpire who turned down one of his appeals. It was a look that would make any long-time student of the game question if they knew anything at all. And the result was that the next time a Warne appeal would come across the umpire's desk, he was more disposed to answer in the affirmative.

Then there were the off-field dramas. I thought he'd thrown away his career when a British nurse accused him of 'harassing' her with 'dirty talk' in 2000. The incident ended Warne's tenure as vice-captain and robbed him of any chance of becoming captain. When he spoke with Mike Munro on *A Current Affair* about the subject, it gave us an insight into the Warne brain. He started the interview by denying the claims made by the nurse, Ms Wright, that he'd harassed her with explicit phone calls. He said he would never harass anybody.

Warne: 'There was a bit of dirty talk, and she did talk dirty to me and I was reciprocating with her.'

And then: 'It was probably the wrong thing to do but I thought it was a private matter. I didn't think it was going to become public and now that it has become public I suppose it is a mistake. If it had stayed private then it wasn't a mistake.'

But as usual, as soon as someone put a ball in his hand and he started turning it at right angles, all of his off-field dramas faded into oblivion.

McGrath would leave Test cricket after Sydney with 563 wickets at 21, while Warne walked away with 708 at 25. At the time of retirement, McGrath was third on the list of all-time wicket-takers. And Warne was number one.

Australia was on autopilot for the Fourth Test in Melbourne, winning by an innings and 99 runs. On Boxing Day, 89,000 had packed into the MCG to say goodbye to Warne and McGrath. Then Justin Langer rose early on New Year's Day 2007 and said he was heading off too. The greatest era in the history of Australian cricket had reached its natural conclusion. How any of them would be able to concentrate on that final Test and bury England for the temerity of 2005 was anyone's guess, but they got the job done and walked away with a 10-wicket victory and a 5–nil whitewash.

Warne, McGrath and Langer had the honour of writing their own farewell. Tragedy followed the next year, with Jane McGrath's passing. Not only did this cause an unprecedented outpouring of grief among cricket fans, but also from every Australian grateful for what she did to raise awareness for breast cancer. Every year, during the Sydney Test, Jane McGrath Day raises millions of dollars to fund breast care nurses throughout Australia.

No helmet

As far as life went, I'd finally hit a smooth patch. Repeats of *Wilfred* were far out-rating the first run and DVD sales were surprisingly strong. Amanda and I made a pilot for a new sitcom called *Lowdown* based on the life of a tabloid journalist and we had bites from networks who wanted to turn it into a series.

Meanwhile, the AFI nominations came out; *Wilfred* was nominated for Best Comedy and I was nominated for Best Performance in a Comedy, which probably meant more to me than it should have. But when the big night came around, I was only focused on Geoffrey's jokes. In my mind, the embarrassment of them not working would outweigh any joy I'd get from walking away with a trophy. I didn't think we were going to win anyway. But the jokes worked. I lip-synced along as Geoffrey spoke. Then came the Best Comedy category – which *Wilfred* won. Then came the Best Performance in a Comedy category ...

The major benefit of winning that award was that it stopped me feeling sorry for myself. Or, if I did start moping around, I'd quickly remind myself of my good fortune and snap out of it. This new, mature, even-headed approach to the world lasted a full five days before I found myself alone in a Brisbane hotel room, trying not to hear the couple next door loudly fornicating. I would be facing someone bowling at me in the high 140s without modern padding or a helmet the following day, and the moaning coming through the walls was distracting me from imagining all the ways it could go horribly wrong.

I wondered who the bowler would be. The producers would have locked in someone by now or they wouldn't have flown me to Brisbane. The obvious choice would be Brett Lee, but he'd likely be expensive. Mitchell Johnson turning up would be scary. I knew how to get away from a right-arm delivery, but I might find myself boxed in with a left-armer. I didn't think it would be McGrath – it'd been a while since he'd clocked over 140 km/h and speed was important to replicate Larwood and Bodyline. Maybe Gillespie could still get there. Tait? It occurred to me that I hadn't made a will, but it was too late to worry about that. All week, the producers had asked me if I was 'comfortable' with what was about to happen. It was a moot point. If I didn't do it, the doco we'd spent more than 18 months making would end in a whimper. Besides, Hamish and Andy would've done it. I put earplugs in. They didn't block out what was happening next door.

Next day, I padded up with modern protective equipment and a helmet and went out to the middle of Allan Border Field and started facing grade bowlers to get my eye in. I laid bat on ball a few times and managed to avoid the short stuff. After about 20 minutes, the director told me it was time to take my helmet off and change into the purely decorative leg and finger guards they used for 'protection' in the 1930s. So it was happening. Instead of getting nervous, I suddenly felt like I could sleep 15 hours straight. The crew all thought I was handling the situation well, but being overwhelmed with fatigue is how my body processes terror.

When I walked out of the change room, I saw a white Mercedes pull up in the car park and tried to convince myself that the guy in the front passenger seat, with the blond hair and wraparound sunnies, was Andy Bichel. Great bowler. Workhorse. Ten kilometres slower than Brett Lee. But when the door opened, the figure that emerged was familiar to any cricket fan. He was wearing his Australian creams as he rotated his body from side to side to loosen his back before catching my eye.

'Adam!' he said, bearing those perfect teeth.

'Hi, Brett,' I said. 'Great to meet you.'

We shook hands. I tried to be super nice to him in the hope that it might knock a few k's off his pace. But I think it just came across as desperate. The cameras were all set up and I went into the middle wearing the vintage leg and finger 'guards' and carrying my smaller bat, handcrafted to the dimensions of the bat Bradman used: 108 mm wide, which is still standard today, but with 20 mm edges. The difference between Bradman's bat and Dave Warner's Kaboom bat is that the edges and depth of Bradman's were half the size. Even though the weights of bats haven't changed, there's a larger sweet spot. Bradman may have averaged 120 with the Kaboom. But it wasn't relevant for me because my bat was merely a prop. My job was to avoid the ball at all costs. The fielders were all lovely to me. So was the wicketkeeper. You know you're in trouble when an Australian wicketkeeper is being lovely to you.

Lee was now at the top of his run, staring at me as he flicked the ball from hand to hand. The warmth that was in his eyes when he first greeted me had gone and he was ready to do his job. He bowed his head like a martial artist before a fight, then started charging toward the wicket. I tried to remember what Matthew Hayden, John Hastings, Neil Buszard, the guy with the eye tracker and everyone else said about watching the ball ... but I was too distracted by who was carrying it, a freak of nature who once sent down a delivery at over 160 km/h.

When he arrived at the wicket and released the ball, I didn't see it until it was five metres in front of my face. But I was able to get inside it as it fizzed past my ear. For the rest of the over, my modus operandi was to get away from each delivery without looking like I was *running* away. I think I almost managed it by getting inside and outside the line for the next four balls. Everything had gone to plan in that I was humiliated but alive. But when Brett Lee sent down his final delivery, I didn't see it at the same point as I'd seen the others and unwittingly stepped into its path. It wasn't until the ball was 60 cm from my skull that I finally sighted it. I didn't have time to move my feet. The only option was to kink my neck back as far as possible.

So I did.

The ball sailed millimetres past my nose, leaving a puff of wind in its wake.

I'd done as I was told – I'd just managed to keep my eye on the ball – and that's what saved my life.

That was it for me. As a performer, I'd always cared whether a director had got the shot they needed, but not after that. After that, I was done. And I said as much in my best Christian Bale voice. The director told me to keep my 1930s-style pants on because he had more than enough footage anyway and he called a wrap on the shoot.

Brett Lee shook my hand. 'Mate,' he said, 'I would *not* have done that.'

Epilogue

I'm envious of people who say they don't have regrets. I've got a billion.

I used to think all the time I spent watching cricket was one of them. If only I'd filled some of those hours reading classic literature or taking in great cinema or music, maybe I'd be a more rounded person. Then again, cricket gave my life context and a timeline. For instance, I know when my voice broke because it happened quickly and harshly during the 1985 Ashes tour of England, specifically the Sixth Test, in which Graeme Wood scored a century and England won by eight wickets. I got a flat-top haircut on the day Dean Jones scored 184 not out at the SCG against England in January 1987. I got my first girlfriend during a ten-wicket win against England in the First Test in Brisbane, in 1990. I realised that relationship was over 10 weeks later during a nine-wicket Australian win in the Fifth Test at the WACA, in which Craig McDermott took 11 wickets for the match and Australia retained the Ashes 3–nil. I moved to Melbourne on the night of the opening ceremony of the 1996 World Cup. And I got married just before the Third Test against India in 2003, which Australia won by nine wickets and Ricky Ponting scored 257.

I've been in a relationship with the 11 men wearing Baggy Green caps over bad haircuts for more than 40 years. They've seen me through success and failure, happiness and despair, love and death. Mostly we grieved separately, but occasionally we suffered together – like when Tony Greig came on national television from his backyard on 9 November 2012 to tell us why he hadn't been in the commentary box that day.

Mark Nicholas: 'Big fella, give us an update on your situation because there's vast interest everywhere in the world, incidentally, not just here in Australia.'

The 6'6" former England captain who had grown up in South Africa stared down the camera with the confidence and strength that had been his hallmark for more than 30 years.

Greig: 'Well, I mean, look, it's not good. Mark, the truth is I've got lung cancer. And it's now just a question of what they can do. And I had a very important meeting with my doctor this morning and I'm going in on Monday for a Tuesday operation. So I'll be in hospital for at least a week. And then, we'll start the fight back after that. Once we've done this operation ... the plan is to embark upon some chemotherapy to see if we can, you know, make a bit of a dent in this little bit of a setback that I've had.'

And then the always stoic, always courageous Greig started to show some vulnerability.

Greig: 'You guys will all face it one day, I'm sure, but you have no idea how much one misses getting to the cricket on a day like today when you've been doing it for 33 years. It's absolutely unbelievable. Even my little bloke, who came home from school today, said, "Dad, what are you doing at home? I mean, you shouldn't be here." You know, so it takes a little bit of getting used to, and I'm sure it's going to get worse as the Test unfolds.'

Nicholas: 'Well, it's just beautiful to see you on the screen and to hear your voice. We wish you well. And I don't just mean those of us sitting in here. I mean a lot of people around the world who followed you for many years and are huge admirers of yours, you have a great power base behind you, mate. Good luck with it.'

And that's when Tony paused, his voice slightly quivering.

Greig: 'Thank you very much.'

A month later, Amanda and I were on holiday in South Africa, lining up to take a connecting flight from Johannesburg to Cape Town, when news broke that Tony Greig had died of a heart attack. One by one, the passengers looked up to see the mute images accompanied by a chyron on the TV screen hanging from the departure lounge wall. There were gasps, exclamations, phone calls to friends to share the news. Mark Nicholas was right. He meant so much to all of us.

I ended this book in 2007 because that's when my great romance with Australian cricket finished. I didn't feel comfortable hero-worshipping guys my own age – or, God forbid, younger. I was happy to follow them, applaud them, but it'd be uncomfortable for everyone if I allowed them to have any greater influence on my life than that.

In any case, after 2007 the Australian men's team started its slow decline. Ponting relinquished his captaincy duties after Australia was bundled out in the quarterfinals of the 2011 World Cup. Michael Clarke took over and the results were up and down. Clarke was tactically brilliant. His instincts for bowling changes and field placements and when to declare were aggressive and exciting and made you love watching the game. But the teams Clarke led were less gifted compared to the immortals Taylor, Waugh and Ponting had at their disposal, and there were question marks over the new skipper's management skills.

During his tenure, stories emerged of fallings-out between Clarke and his senior players. Mitchell Johnson later said cliques had developed in the team and the atmosphere was toxic. 'It wasn't a very enjoyable place to be and you're supposed to be enjoying yourself when you're playing for your country,' Johnson told

Fox Sports News. 'It was a pretty bad experience, bad time. A couple of us didn't want to play.'

Clarke's nadir was 'Homeworkgate'. Midway through Australia's tour to India in 2013, coach Mickey Arthur asked each member of the team to write down three ways in which the team could improve and three ways in which players could improve as individuals. Shane Watson, Usman Khawaja, Mitchell Johnson and James Pattinson all failed to complete the task, so Arthur and Clarke suspended them for the next Test, describing the penalty as a 'line in the sand' following a gradual decline in disciplinary standards off the field. The incident caused a massive backlash from former legends and prematurely ended Arthur's tenure as coach. India won the series 4–nil.

Darren Lehmann took over as coach for the 2013 Ashes tour of England and Mitchell Johnson was banished to Western Australia to work on his action with Dennis Lillee. Dave Warner punched Joe Root in a pub in Birmingham and we lost the Ashes 3–nil. There was no way you'd tip Australia to win back the Ashes in the return series at home five months later. But Lillee sprinkled his magic stardust over Johnson and the big quick unleashed the most brutal season of fast bowling in the history of Australian Test cricket. OK, maybe Thommo in 1974–75 was just as terrifying. Kevin Pietersen said he was 'petrified' of Johnson, and Jonathan Trott said facing Johnson was like facing a firing squad.

By the end of the series, Johnson had taken 37 wickets at 13.

Clarke retired after Australia's sterling win in the 2015 World Cup and handed the captaincy over to Steve Smith, who'd gone from almost forgettable to the next Bradman.

In 2016, Amanda and I moved to the cricketless, and therefore Godless, city of Los Angeles. The US version of *Wilfred*, starring Elijah Wood, had finished its four-season run on FX and there was interest in a US format of *Lowdown*, the show Amanda and I created for the ABC.

Before I left, I sent my new US manager, Zack, a script I'd written called *Mr Black*, a dark comedy about a dying father whose final wish was to break up the relationship between his daughter and her wimpy boyfriend. Amanda was already in LA and I was moving the last of our stuff into storage when I got a call from Zack, saying that Kelsey Grammer had read the script and wanted to play the role of Mr Black. It was just the kind of soft landing I needed to make it in a new country. Then, while I was in a taxi to the airport, Zack called again to say Kelsey was out because he wanted to produce the show and Zack's management company, which was also a production house, wanted to hold on to production rights.

'OK,' I said, disappointed, but confident Zack knew what he was doing.

Zack said he was about to hand the script to a

client of his called Charlie Sheen. Alright, I had slight reservations about Charlie Sheen on the grounds that he was Charlie Sheen, but he had impeccable comic timing, and I looked forward to the financial benefits that came with being involved in one of his projects.

I arrived at LAX in late January 2016. The first person to call on my new US cell phone was Zack. 'Charlie's passed,' he said. 'But it's fine. We've attached a guy called Gavin McInnes. He's hilarious. He's a real-life Mr Black!' Zack sent me a link to a feature film Gavin had starred in. The first scene showed him working diligently at a computer, then getting up to reveal he was completely without pants – his naked penis dangling lifelessly in front of the screen. It's an old joke, but the way he handled it made me laugh. Maybe he was the guy. Then I googled him and found he'd pivoted from being the co-founder of Vice Media to becoming an actor, comedian and then a Fox and Friends pundit. I didn't really love the sound of that ... but maybe Zack was right. He was the real-life Mr Black.

New York–based Gavin flew out to LA and we spent a week trying to sell the show to networks. Our first pitch was on a Monday morning at 10 and I asked Gavin to meet me at my place in West Hollywood at 9. He arrived at 7.30 am. I was still in my pyjamas.

'Is this your house?' he said, frowning in the doorway.

I said it was. He walked in, looked around, and made the two-thumbs-down signal before blowing a big raspberry. I thought that was extreme, but figured he must be so rich after selling his share of Vice Media that he wasn't used to a regular house. Then he saw our cats and told me he hated cats. I told him there was a café down the road, to get himself a coffee, and that I didn't want to see him for at least an hour. Off he went.

After the shaky start, Gavin and I got on fine. He came across as a smart and funny anarchist. I didn't think he believed most of the crap that came out of his mouth. I thought he was just a shock comic. Then one afternoon between pitches he told me how he'd shifted from being progressive to conservative after September 11, and that he no longer related to the person he was. He now described himself as a 'Western chauvinist' with an anti-white-guilt agenda.

Gavin told me he'd started an organisation called the Proud Boys. He talked about it a lot, but all I retained was that it was *verboten* for its members to wank. This triggered me a bit as it brought back memories of Brisbane Grammar and the wanking police. In my mind, Gavin was building an army of wanking police.

The pitching went badly. I was used to pitching in LA and had sold shows and come close with others. Normally it's a pleasant experience. Not this time. In every pitch, Gavin would say something inappropriate and I'd try to tap dance out of it. When we were travelling from one pitch to another, it was clear Zack had fallen in love with Gavin. They'd sit in the front of Zack's BMW, and Gavin would talk about how 'obsessed' Jews were with the Holocaust: 'I know it was bad – don't get me wrong, I'm not pro-Holocaust.' And Zack, who was Jewish, would laugh heartily. And I'd be in the back seat wondering what world I was in.

Our final pitch ended in a wall of ashen faces when Gavin got into a debate with an executive who'd disagreed with Gavin's contention that 'no means no' was 'puritanism'. Afterwards, Zack tried to set up a time with Gavin to 'hang' with him in New York and Gavin stared at him with a confused look on his face before getting into his cab. He then wound down the passenger window, called me over and asked if I'd join the Proud Boys. I said 'no'.

The next time I would see Gavin McInnes, he would be on television, leading what had become Donald Trump's favourite right-wing hate group.

Steve Smith's man management might've been different to Clarke's, but not better. That became abundantly clear on the third day of the Third Test in Cape Town in 2018, when he walked past Dave Warner and newcomer Cameron Bancroft having a shifty-looking conversation during the lunch break. He clocked them, said, 'I don't want to know about it', then walked off. Perhaps it was because Smith didn't 'want to know about it' that Bancroft suddenly felt emboldened to scuff the match ball between deliveries with a piece of sandpaper hidden in his palm.

He did this because if one side of the ball is smooth and the other extremely rough, a fast bowler is able to create reverse swing, a phenomenon whereby the trajectory of the ball moves in the opposite direction to what the batter expects. For example, at the point of delivery, a batter might see the bowler grip the ball like they're going to bowl an outswinger and the delivery will end up swinging in toward the batter because the airflow on the damaged side of the ball has become so messy that it forces the ball in the opposite direction. It's a great tactic, and cricket's stakeholders are fine if the fielding side can achieve reverse swing by polishing one side of the ball with their clothing, or even a towel, and allowing the other side to be worn and torn by the natural elements of the game. What is *not* allowed is to fast-track the process by actively damaging the ball with an artificial substance or scuffing it with fingernails or an implement. So when footage flashed up on the big screen at Newlands of Bancroft putting an unidentified object in his pocket after 'polishing' the ball, the crowd murmured with suspicion.

Coach Darren Lehmann immediately radioed 12th man Peter Handscomb to ask Bancroft what was going on. Handscomb ran onto the ground and spoke to Bancroft who, in a state of panic, took the object out of his pocket and put it down the front of his pants. As he did this, the cameras were on him and the object was revealed to be a yellow square of sandpaper. Throughout the history of international cricket, bottle tops, dirt, medical tape, lollies, Vaseline, soft drinks, penknives, lip balm and sunscreen have all been used to damage one side of a cricket ball to try to achieve reverse swing. In 2013, future South African captain Faf du Plessis was fined for rubbing the ball up and down his zipper during a game against Pakistan. Perhaps the most brazen act of ball tampering was Pakistan's Shahid Afridi biting the ball, as if it were an apple, during a T20 match against Australia in 2010. But the broader Australian population doesn't really care about the wicked history of this once 'genteel' game – all they saw was footage of one of their guys cheating.

I was in LA and saw what had happened before Australia had woken up. Then I sat back and watched its citizenry go into meltdown. For a hundred years, the Australian men's cricket team had been Australia's representatives in the world, and our shame in them manifested as shame in ourselves. We didn't know who we were anymore.

Perhaps the most humiliating moment was the *NT News* front-page photo of Bancroft putting the sandpaper into his underpants and the accompanying headline: 'WHY I'VE GOT SOME STICKY NEAR MY DICKY'.

Smith and Warner both received 12-month bans from the game while Bancroft was ineligible to play for nine months. Smith wouldn't be able to captain Australia for two years while Warner was barred from ever holding a leadership position in the national side again. Tim Paine was made captain for the final Test in South Africa. He would make a solid captain. He wasn't a cricketing prodigy like Smith and Ponting, nor a tactician like Clarke or Taylor, nor an icon like Border or Waugh. He was just a decent guy who understood pain after an unspeakably bad run of injuries. A good keeper and a technically correct old-school batter. Most of all, he was a mature human.

With Paine at the wheel, we haven't been a world-beating team, but we've been steady and had some nice wins along the way – namely, the 2019 Ashes in which Smith was able to rehabilitate his reputation by crunching 774 runs at an average of 110.

It was an uncomfortable summer for Smith, where he was consistently booed by English crowds during Australia's run into the semifinals of the World Cup and then again in the opening stages of the Ashes.

Dave Warner copped it as well with the Barmy Army repurposing Pink Floyd's *Another Brick in the Wall* to let Warner know how they felt about him.

He still needs some education,
He still needs some self-control,
No gold sandpaper in his pocket

Warner, leave those balls alone
Hey, Warner, leave those balls alone
All in all he's just another cheat like them all ...

Unlike Smith, Warner wasn't able to erase his misdoings by sheer weight of runs. When Smith was dismissed for 23 in the last Test at The Oval, it was the first time in the series he'd made less than 80. He finished with one double century, two hundreds and two fifties. As he made his way off the field, the boos that had accompanied him all summer turned into cheers. Then fans got out of their seats and gave him a standing ovation.

I'm now back in Australia and grateful for it.

I spent nearly five years in LA. At the time of writing, Amanda is directing a TV series for BBC/HBO. Dad was diagnosed with progressive supranuclear palsy – a condition that causes problems with walking, movement and balance. He still writes beautifully.

I still think of Mum every day. She would have been 80 this year. I marvel at her strength. I got the desire to tell stories and the solid, Germanic work ethic from Dad, and determination and a sense of the absurd from Mum. I'm sorry she lived in a time when women's voices were muzzled and she didn't get a chance to shine as much as she should have.

I saw people talk over her. When that happened, I'd silently will her to keep talking or to shout over her interrupters, but that wasn't her style. My uncle collected a lot of her recipes and her genius as a cook lives on in him. He won't have read this book because of the swearing.

These days when I'm struggling to sleep, I imagine I'm batting for Australia against the might of that 1980s West Indian attack. I walk out just as Allan Border did, staring toward the sun so my eyes adjust to the light. I take guard then elegantly survive the onslaught of Malcolm Marshall and Michael Holding before there's a change and Joel Garner comes on, bowling yorkers. I manage to dig those out too, much to the delight of Tony Greig in the comm box. Colin Croft is always difficult to handle as he delivers the ball so wide of the crease, angling it in at my head. But in the dream I'm able to take a step back and cut Croft on the rise over Roger Harper at gully. Four runs.

Then, once the pacemen are exhausted, I find sweet respite in Viv Richards' darts or the loping off spinners of Harper ... but the truth is, I'm generally asleep by the time Croft comes on.

I'm not going to lose interest in cricket now. I'm in for the long haul. In the words of nineteenth-century County cricketer JH Hardy: 'If I knew I was going to die today, I'd still want to hear the score.'

Acknowledgements

Thank you –

Amanda Brotchie, your multiple reads, structural know-how, story-remembering and high IQ are all greatly appreciated. I know how lucky I am.

Desmond Zwar – the true author in the family. Twenty books and counting.

Delphine Zwar – I miss you, Mum. So much of you is in this book.

My agent of 24 years, Aran Michael, for your dedication and faith.

Bradley Trevor Greive for throwing in judicious comments in between safaris.

The extraordinary team at Hachette for taking a chance on me –

Sophie Hamley
Jacquie Brown
Libby Turner
Emily Lighezzolo

My cricket guys:

Stephen Vagg
Russell Jackson
Lawrie Colliver
Dan Allan
Daniel Brettig

My friend Chris Wallace, who always asked, 'How's that book doing?' And then listened.

Finally, my feline writers' room – Missy and Kaspar Zwar.

Sources

Chapter 1

Australian Cricket, Star Spot, publication date unknown. *Modern Magazines*, Sydney.

'Underarm: The ball that changed cricket', Seven Network, 2018. https://7plus.com.au/underarm-the-ball-that-changed-cricket

A McGregor, *Greg Chappell*, Sydney, Collins, 1985.

Loxton's total recall: Underarms were legitimate, just not the way Trevor Chappell bowled his', *Sydney Morning Herald*, 28 December 2009.

R Craddock, 'Tony Greig slams Brian McKechnie over response to underarm ball', *Daily Telegraph*, 20 November 2008.

Chapter 2

G Baum, 'Simpson one of the greats', *The Age*, 6 February 2006.

D Jones 'Australia's forgotten World Cup win', *Sydney Morning Herald*, 20 January 2017.

J Anderson, 'Simon O'Donnell tells how surviving cancer changed his life', *Herald Sun*, 12 October 2012.

Chapter 3

That 1980s Sports Blog, '1989 Ashes: An A to Z of Humiliation', *The Guardian*, 13 September 2019.

'Savour dominance: Border', *The Age*, 9 January 2005.

O Samiuddin, 'The miracle of '92', *The Cricket Monthly*, November 2014.

P Lutton, 'Sir Ian's beef over Queen gag', *Brisbane Times*, 28 September 2007.

D Brettig, 'Australia look to heal an old wound', ESPNcricinfo, 28 March 2015. https://www.espncricinfo.com/story/daniel-brettig-australia-look-to-heal-an-old-wound-856521

'It wasn't Australia's day', *The Age*, 14 December 2003.

B Eva, 'PSSST: Narrowest victory in test cricket', *Sydney Morning Herald*, 26 January 2013.

Chapter 4

M Coward, *Cricket Beyond the Bazaar,* Sydney, Allen & Unwin, 1990.

S Watson, 'Lessons Learnt from the Greats' podcast, 'Dean Jones on running between the wickets, his father and the importance of networking,' 26 June 2020.

P Kent, 'Great Grand Finals: Allan Langer sings "St George can't play" after 1993 Grand Final between Broncos and Dragons', *Daily Telegraph*, 4 October 2013.

G Baum, 'Selectors spurn Jones for Australia A Team', *The Age*, 30 November 1994.

G Baum, 'Victory Hollow: Taylor', *The Age*, 12 December 1994.

Chapter 5

'Jeff Thomson', ESPNcricinfo, 15 July 2007. https://www.espncricinfo.com/player/jeff-thomson-7946

P Best, 'Rob Stewart: Human Rod Stewart', album review, *Sunday Herald Sun*, 11 March 2001.

P Wilkins, 'Move our match, Waugh urges', *Sydney Morning Herald*, 2 February 1996.

G Baum, 'Australia to forfeit points', *The Age*, 6 February 1996.

'Episode 116: Shane Lee', 'The Betoota Advocate' podcast, 29 June 2020.

'Episode 11: Australia – Damien Fleming', 'The Greatest Season That Was' podcast, 1 August 2019.

B Graham and C de Silva, 'Ian Healy comes clean on cricket's most famous sledge', *Wide World of Sports*, Nine Network, 29 December 2020.

B Graham and C de Silva, 'The oral history of Sri Lanka's treacherous path to cricket's greatest upset', *Wide World of Sports*, Nine Network, 17 March 2021.

Tony Greig, commentator, First Test – Australia v India, Mumbai, *Fox Sports*, 17 March 1996.

Mark Taylor interviewed by Ian Chappell, *Sky Sports*, 17 March 1996.

Chapter 6

A Burnett, 'Caribbean 1999, Pt II: "He'd hit rock bottom"', cricket.com.au, 15 March 2019. https://www.cricket.com.au/news/feature/west-indies-australia-1999-flashback-series-waugh-lara-ambrose-oral-history-second-test-jamaica/2019-03-15

S Warne and M Nicholas, *No Spin*, Sydney, Penguin Books Australia, 2020.

M Knox, 'I may quit, says Warne', *Sydney Morning Herald*, 5 April 1999.

G Pritchard and A Brown, 'Waugh's Insult', *Sun Herald*, 11 April 1999.

'Episode 11: Australia – Damien Fleming', 'The Greatest Season That Was' podcast, 1 August 2019.

Chapter 7

Steve Waugh, *Out of My Comfort Zone: The Autobiography*, Melbourne, Penguin Books Australia, 2006.

Tony Greig and David Gower, commentators, Australia v South Africa Super Six, Leeds, *Wide World of Sports*, Nine Network, 13 June 1999.

'Episode 13: Australia – Tom Moody', 'The Greatest Season That Was' podcast, 18 May 2020.

Chapter 8

Slats – The Michael Slater Story, Michael Slater with Jeff Apter, Sydney, Random House Australia, 2005.

'Enough Rope with Andrew Denton', ABC TV, Episode #3.3, 14 March 2005.

Steve Waugh, *Out of My Comfort Zone: The Autobiography*, Melbourne, Penguin Books Australia, 2006.

'Episode 4: The Final Frontier – Adam Gilchrist', 'The Greatest Season That Was' podcast, 17 January 2021.

A Mallett, *The Diggers' Doctor: The fortunate life of Col. Donald Beard*, Adelaide, Wakefield Press, 2014.

D Bogle, 'Cricket's Other Don', *The Advertiser*, 12 September 2014.

M Cleary, 'Jason Gillespie recalls the weirdest Test innings of all time: and what happened immediately after', *Fox Sports*, 4 September 2017.

Tony Greig, commentator, First Test – Australia v India, Mumbai, *Fox Sports*, 1 March 2001.

D McRae, 'Interview: Michael Slater', *The Guardian*, 22 August 2005.

'5 infamous moments in India versus Australia Test Cricket history', Sports.info, January 2021. https://www.sports.info/article/5-infamous-moments-in-india-vs-australia-test-cricket-history

Chapter 9

R Gould, 'The Ashes 2019: Mark Waugh reveals what made the last Aussie team to win in England so special', *The Daily Telegraph*, 11 August 2019.

Wisden Staff, 'When Langer grabbed Gilchrist "by the neck" during the 2001 Ashes', 25 July 2020. https://wisden.com/stories/when-langer-grabbed-gilchrist-by-the-neck-2001-ashes

J Cadzow, 'Can Justin Langer save Australian men's cricket?', *Sydney Morning Herald*, 26 January 2019.

T Elbra, 'Steve Waugh wrong to drop Shane Warne in moment that began feud, Mark Taylor says', *Wide World of Sports*, Nine Network, 24 May 2020.

A Wu, 'The calf, the dive and that raised bat: Steve Waugh's 2001 medical miracle', *The Age*, 10 September 2019.

J Cadzow, 'Can Justin Langer Save Australian Men's Cricket?', *Sydney Morning Herald*, 26 January 2019.

G Haigh, 'Game is over for Slater', *The Age*, 9 June 2004.

D McRae, 'Interview: Michael Slater', *The Guardian*, 22 August 2005.

Steve Waugh, *Out of My Comfort Zone: The Autobiography*, Melbourne, Penguin Books Australia, 2006.

Chapter 10

R Das, 'On this day: Steve Waugh's resistance brought about a new era in Australian cricket', Crickxtasy.com, 21 April 2020. https://www.cricxtasy.com/on-this-day-steve-waughs-resistance-brought-about-a-new-era-in-australian-cricket/

Allan Border and Tony Cozier, commentators, Third Test – Australia v West Indies, Trinidad, *Sky Sports*, 21 April 1995.

'Steve Waugh: A Perfect Day', Documentary, Roadshow Entertainment, 19 February 2003.

Steve Waugh, *Out of My Comfort Zone: The Autobiography*, Melbourne, Penguin Books Australia, 2006.

Tony Greig, commentator, Fifth Ashes Test, Sydney, *Wide World of Sports*, Nine Network, 3 January 2003.

Jonathan Agnew, commentator, Fifth Ashes Test, Sydney, *ABC Grandstand*, 3 January 2003.

Chapter 11

J Hotten, 'Ashes 2005: The inside story of the greatest series', *Wisden*, 16 March 2020.

C Saltau, '"We Were a Bit Cocky": inside the closest Test in Ashes history', *Sydney Morning Herald*, 31 July 2019.

'2005 Ashes', Mark Nicholas interviewing Ricky Ponting, Channel 4, 4 August 2005.

N Evershed, 'Richie Benaud's best quotes', *The Guardian*, 10 April 2015.

M Williamson, 'Today, Australians know how it felt to be English', ESPNcricinfo, 14 September 2005. https://www.espncricinfo.com/story/today-australians-know-how-it-felt-to-be-english-219202

Chapter 12

G Watson, 'Bodyline: 80 years of cricket's greatest controversy', BBC, 16 January 2013. https://www.bbc.com/news/uk-england-nottinghamshire-21013615

P Kelso, 'England pass screen test', *The Guardian*, 23 November 2002.

A Sengupta, 'The Bodyline cables: Australian Board sends the infamous protest message to MCC', cricketcountry.com, 18 January 2017. https://www.cricketcountry.com/articles/the-bodyline-cables-australian-board-sends-the-infamous-protest-message-to-mcc-86804

M Williamson, 'The Ball of the Century', espncricinfo.com, 3 August 2013. https://www.espncricinfo.com/story/rewind-to-1993-the-ball-of-the-century-657991

A Zwar, 'Ten Questions with Adam Zwar: Stuart MacGill' podcast, 4 January 2018.

Epilogue

AAP, 'Johnson "didn't want to play" amid "toxic" culture of Michael Clarke's reign', *The Guardian,* 27 October 2016.

M Smith, 'England were "scared" of Mitch: KP', cricket.com.au, 9 October 2014. https://www.cricket.com.au/news/kevin-pietersen-says-england-were-scared-of-mitchell-johnson-during-ashes-series/2014-10-09

'Steve Smith admits he said "I don't want to know about it" during ball-tampering saga', abc.net.au, 21 December 2018. https://www.abc.net.au/news/2018-12-21/steve-smith-admits-to-failing-as-australian-captain/10646558

C Barrett, '"What the f--- is going on?" The words that cleared Darren Lehmann', *Sydney Morning Herald*, 28 March 2018.

hachette
AUSTRALIA

If you would like to find out more about Hachette Australia, our authors, upcoming events and new releases you can visit our website or our social media channels:

hachette.com.au
HachetteAustralia
HachetteAus